VINTAGE HOLLYWOOD KNITS

Published in the United Kingdom in 2015 by
Pavilion
1 Gower Street
London
WC1E 6HD

ISBN 978-1-91049-608-4

A CIP catalogue record for this book is available from the British Library.

10 9 8 7 6 5 4 3 2 1

Reproduction by Tag Publishing, UK
Printed and bound by 1010 Printing International Ltd, China

This book can be ordered direct from the publisher at www.pavilionbooks.com

Bill Gibb

VINTAGE
HOLLYWOOD

Knit 20 glamorous
sweaters as worn
by the stars
KNITS

PAVILION

Contents

Introduction

All the patterns in this book were inspired by iconic shots of screen stars from vintage Hollywood, reinterpreted by the legendary fashion designer Bill Gibb (see right) in 1987. This double treasure trove of bygone glamour has been updated so that today's vintage-loving fashionistas can knit them with modern yarns. Knits are often used in movies set in earlier eras. For example, costume designer Sandy Powell based her sweater design for Hugo in the film *Hugo* (2011) on an original, hand dying the yarn to achieve a period feel to the colours and choosing an authentically scratchy wool, rather than a softer, more contemporary yarn. Yarn suggestions in this book are based on comfort and ease of knitting, rather than authenticity, however.

Twiggy knitting on the set of *The Boyfriend* (1971), a musical set in the theatrical world of the 1920s at the start of the talkies. Chunky knits with large needles were very fashionable in the 1960s and early 1970s.

Bill Gibb
1943 – 1988

Scottish fashion designer Bill Gibb's designs were inspired by nature – his signature was a stylized bee. Gibb's intricately patterned knitwear, often designed with close friend Kaffe Fassett, featured complicated colour palettes that included mustard, lime green and purple, and caramel, cream and duck egg blue with flecks of gold lurex.

He produced designs for the Alice Paul boutique and mass market label Baccarat, as well as for his own label. He was voted Vogue's designer of the year in 1970 for a collection that mixed plaids with brightly patterned knitwear. Twiggy wore a Bill Gibb dress to the premiere of her movie *The Boyfriend* in 1971, bringing his designs to international attention. His work has been a great influence on today's designers, including Christopher Bailey, John Galliano and Giles Deacon.

Screen Yarns

From the early silent movies to the latest romcom, costume designers have come up with memorable knitwear designs that reflect the wearer's character and the film's story. Certain garments end up being associated with particular eras or stars. For example, Clara Bow popularized the cloche hat in the 1920s and some knitted versions have been named after her.

Sweaters for women feature in a range of roles, but the starring one is sexy dame. Lana Turner was nicknamed 'The Sweater Girl' by movie magazines after her first brief film appearance as murder victim Mary Clay at the start of a 1937 film *They Won't Forget*. And in the 1940s and 50s, stars such as Jane Russell and Jayne Mansfield sported tight sweaters over cone-shaped brassieres and were also called sweater girls. Later, a 30s'-style short-sleeved sweater was part of Faye Dunaway's trendsetting period-influenced wardrobe in her role as Bonnie Parker in *Bonnie and Clyde* (1967). The costume designer for the film, Theadora van Runkle, won an Academy award for her work on that film.

Sweater girl Rita Hayworth wears a fitted top in a 1940s design that adds a sexy glamour to the usually prim cardigan.

Screen Yarns

The boat-necked close-fitting top sported by Hollywood siren Dorothy Lamour on page 64 is a typical sweater girl knit.

Male stars are seen in everything from macho sporting sweaters, like the one worn by Cary Grant on page 47, to Johnny Depp cross-dressing in a sweet little angora cardigan in *Ed Wood* (1994). Bookish educators like Steve Macinter (Steve Allen) in *College Confidential* (1960) wear cardigans, while dashing action heroes drape their sweaters over their shoulders. Some movie stars such as Roger Moore modelled for knitting patterns before they found fame on screen.

Knitting for pets gets a moment on screen too. In *Shall We Dance* (1937) musical dancing star Linda Keene (Ginger Rogers) is seen on a ship's deck sitting next to lovestruck Russian ballet star Petrov (Fred Astaire), who followed her onto the ocean liner. She is wielding knitting needles and working on a dog's coat. This starts a rumour that she is pregnant, and a mortified Linda jumps ship aboard a mail plane.

A cosy cardigan sported by Steve Allen in *College Confidential* (1960) is perfect for his role as a mild-manned professor who stumbles into a scandal when his academic research on student's sex habits results in media attention and a legal battle.

'Reel' Knitters

Although some movie stars seen knitting on screen hold their needles in such a way that its obvious they don't knit, the role call of actors who knit in real life is a long one, ranging from vintage movie stars such as Mary Pickford and Bette Davis to modern celebrities such as Goldie Hawn, Julia Roberts and Sarah Jessica Parker. Many stars find that the hobby is a relaxing and productive way to pass the time while waiting for a call to go on set.

The fashion for knitting among film stars has even made its way into movie

Katharine Hepburn knitting between scenes while filming *Sylvia Scarlett* (1936), her first film with Cary Grant as co-star.

Cary Grant at the War Relief charity knitting circle in *Mr Lucky* (1943). In later scenes he overcomes his initial reluctance and learns to knit.

scripts. In *Raising Helen* (2004), when the doorbell rings at Jenny (Joan Cusack) and Ed (Kevin Kilner) Portman's home, Ed comments: "Maybe it's a celebrity, coming to knit with you."

During the black and white movie era men are usually shown holding the yarn ball like Walter Pidgeon for his screen wife Greer Garson in *Mrs Miniver* (1942), or helping with yarn winding, like Johnny Haines (Wallace MacDonald) in *His Foreign Wife* (1927). Cary Grant in *Mr Lucky* (see above and page 14) is a comedic exception. However, today some male stars knit on set or on screen. David Arquette, Ryan Gosling and Russell Crowe are all said to wield the needles.

Knit Flicks

For knitters, spotting some needle action on screen is a true treat. From silent movies to the latest releases, there are an astonishing number of clips that click. Here are a few yarn-filled movie moments to get you started.

Marilyn Monroe knitting in *Let's Make Love* (1960), seen here with co-star Yves Montand.

THE BAT (1926)
Nothing can faze an obsessive knitter. Writer Cornelia van Gorder (Emily Fitzroy) knits in most scenes while caped killer The Bat murders her house guests one by one.

CITY LIGHTS (1931)
If you have nightmares about your work unravelling this might not be the movie for you. The blind flower girl (Virginia Cherrill) asks The Tramp (Charlie Chaplin) to hold a skein of yarn for her, and then ends up reeling in a loose thread from his underwear so that it slowly unravels.

MR. LUCKY (1943)
Knitting brings out the best in people. Gambler and rogue Joe Adams/Joe Bascopolous (Cary Grant) joins a War Relief charity with the aim

of swindling it, but falling in love with a glamorous co-worker and being taught to knit by an elderly volunteer reforms him.

STATE OF THE UNION
(1948)
Expert knitters are renowned for being able to knit while watching TV or making conversation. Katherine Hepburn takes this skill up a level, knitting on an aeroplane while pilot Spencer Tracy performs acrobatic stunts.

PHONE CALL FROM A STRANGER (1952)
Here's one for the sock knitters – bedridden widow Marie Hoke (Bette Davis) uses dpns (double-pointed needles) to make some socks. Bette was a keen knitter off-screen too.

LET'S MAKE LOVE (1960)
Giving away the secret addiction of many actors, off Broadway actress Amanda Dell (Marilyn Monroe) is seen knitting while waiting to go on stage. Is it the beautiful cable sweater she wears in the scene where she sings My Heart Belongs to Daddy?

BREAKFAST AT TIFFANY'S
(1961)
Does your knitting ever get out of control? Holly Golightly (Audrey Hepburn) knits a mysterious long red item and comments that her instructions may have been mixed with some house plans. "I've taken up knitting…I'm a little nervous about it. Jose brought up the blueprints for a new ranch house he's building. I have this strange feeling that the blueprints and my knitting instructions got switched. I may be knitting a ranch house." Knowing Holly, she probably didn't bother to make a tension swatch.

HALLOWEEN (1978)
Knitting can be good for you in so many ways. In this horror flick, a handy needle serves as a defence weapon. Laurie (Jamie Lee Curtis) uses them to fend off scary killer Michael Myers (Nick Castle).

THE DEER HUNTER (1978)
Making a sweater to celebrate the connection with your man is a classic rite of passage for knitters. In this movie, Linda (Meryl Streep) knits a sweater for fiancé Nick (Christopher Walken).

BRIDGET JONES'S DIARY
(2001)
The Christmas sweater with a kitsch motif now has its own day to raise money for charity and is worn with pride, or at least joy. In the 90s, wearers were embarrassed rather than proud of the questionable taste of the designs. Mr Darcy (Colin Firth) sheepishly sports a gifted reindeer sweater at a Boxing Day party.

And perhaps the ultimate knitting movie would be set in a yarn store. The screenplay of the novel *The Friday Night Knitting Club* is reportedly in development, with Julia Roberts as the store owner.

Vilma Bánky

MEASUREMENTS

To fit bust:
81 (86, 91, 97, 102)cm
32 (34, 36, 38, 40)in

Actual measurements:
90 (95, 101, 106, 112)cm

Length to shoulders:
66 (67, 68, 69, 70)cm

See schematic for full measurements.

MATERIALS

Rowan Cotton Glacé (50g balls)
   7 (7, 8, 8, 9) balls in main
      colour A
   1 ball of each in contrast
      colours B and C
A pair each of 3.25mm (UK 10)
   and 4mm (UK 8) knitting needles
Stitch holders
Locking stitch marker

TENSION

22 sts and 30 rows to 10cm
over st st using 4mm needles.

Fly the flag with this longline cotton V-necked slipover worked in stocking stitch. The red, white and blue flag motif is worked from a simple chart and the welts are trimmed with garter-stitch stripes in the same contrast colours.

BACK

Using 3.25mm needles and A, cast on 99 (105, 111, 117, 123) sts.
Row 1 (RS): K1, *p1, k1; rep from * to end.
Row 2 (WS): P1, *k1, p1; rep from * to end.
Rep these 2 rows once more.
Row 5: Using B, k to end.
Row 6: Using B, as row 2.
Row 7: Using B, as row 1.
Row 8: Using A, p to end.
Row 9: Using A, as row 1.
Row 10: Using C, p to end.
Rows 11 and 12: Using C, as rows 1 and 2.
Row 13: Using A, k to end.
Row 14: Using A, as row 2.
Rows 15-18: Using A, rep rows 1 and 2 twice.
Change to 4mm needles.
Using A only and beg with a RS knit row, work in st st until back measures 47cm from cast-on edge ending with a WS row.
Shape armhole
Cast off 4 (5, 6, 7, 8) sts at beg of next 2 rows. 91 (95, 99, 103, 107) sts
Dec 1 st at each end of next and every foll alt row until 75 (77, 79, 81, 83) sts remain.
Work straight until armhole measures 17 (18, 19, 20, 21)cm from beg of shaping, ending with a WS row.

Shape neck
Next row (RS): K19 (20, 20, 21, 21), turn and leave remaining sts on a stitch holder.
Work on first set of sts as folls:
Next row (WS): Cast off 2 sts, p to end.
Next row: Cast off 8 (8, 8, 9, 9) sts, k to end.
Next row: Cast off 2 sts, p to end.
7 (8, 8, 8, 8) sts
Cast off.
Return to remaining sts.
With RS facing, leaving first 37 (37, 39, 39, 41) sts on holder, join A to next st and k to end of row.
K 1 row, then complete to match first side of neck, reversing all shaping.

FRONT

Work as given for back until front measures 31.5cm from cast-on edge, ending with a p row.
Commence motif working the intarsia method, joining and cutting colours as needed, using separate small balls of yarn for each area of colour and twisting yarns together when changing colour to avoid making a hole.
Reading odd numbered (k) rows from right to left and even numbered (p) rows from left to right, proceed to position patt from chart as follows:

Vilma Bánky

Row 1 (RS): K15 (18, 21, 24, 27)A, working from chart k13A, 2B, 39A, 2B, 13A, then with A k15 (18, 21, 24, 27).
Row 2 (WS): P15 (18, 21, 24, 27)A, working from chart p14A, 2B, 37A, 2B, 14A, then with A, p15 (18, 21, 24, 27).
Continue working from chart in this way until row 46 has been completed.

Shape armhole

Cast off 4 (5, 6, 7, 8) sts at beg of next 2 rows. 91 (95, 99, 103, 107) sts
Dec 1 st at each end of next and every foll alt row until 85 (89, 93, 97, 101) sts remain, ending with a WS row.

Shape neck

Next row: K2tog, k40 (42, 44, 46, 48), turn and leave remaining sts on a stitch holder.
Work on first set of sts as follows:
Work 1 row.
Dec 1 st at armhole edge as before and **at the same time** dec 1 st at neck edge on next and every foll alt row until 33 sts remain.
Keeping armhole edge straight, continue dec 1 st at neck edge as before until 15 (16, 16, 17, 17) sts remain.
Work straight until front measures same as back to shoulder, ending at armhole edge.

Shape shoulder

Cast off 8 (8, 8, 9, 9) sts at beg of next row.
Work 1 row. Cast off.
Return to remaining sts.
With RS facing, slip first st onto a safety-pin, join A to next st, then k to last 2 sts, k2tog.
Work 1 row, then complete to match first side of neck, reversing all shaping.

FRONT

A Main colour
B Contrast colour
C Contrast colour

NECKBAND

Join right shoulder seam.

With RS facing and using 3.25mm needles and A, pick up and k50 (52, 54, 56, 58) sts down left side of front neck, k the st from safety-pin and mark this st with a locking stitch marker to denote centre st, pick up and k50 (52, 54, 56, 58) sts up right side of front neck and 5 sts down right side of back neck, decreasing 1 st at centre k the sts from back neck holder, then pick up and k5 sts up left side of back neck.
147 (151, 157, 161, 167) sts

Row 1 (WS): Using A, [k1, p1] to within 2 sts of centre st, skpo, p centre st, k2tog, [p1, k1] to end.

Row 2 (RS): Using A, rib to within 2 sts of centre st, skpo, k centre st, k2tog, rib to end.

Row 3: Using B, p to within 2 sts of centre st, p2tog, p centre st, p2tog tbl, p to end.

Row 4: Using B, as row 2.

Row 5: Using B, as row 1.

Row 6: Using A, k to within 2 sts of centre st, k2tog tbl, k centre st, k2tog, k to end.

Row 7: Using A, as row 1.

Row 8: Using C, as row 6.

Row 9: Using C, as row 1.

Row 10: Using C, as row 2.

Row 11: Using A, as row 3.

Using A, cast off loosely in rib.

ARMHOLE BORDERS

Join left shoulder and neckband seam.

With RS facing and using 3.25mm needles and A, pick up and k106 (108, 112, 114, 118) sts evenly round armhole.

Row 1 (WS): Using A, *k1, p1, rep from * to end.

Row 2 (RS): Using B, k to end.

Row 3: Using B, as row 1.

Row 4: Using A, k to end.

Row 5: Using A, as row 1.

Row 6: Using C, k to end.

Row 7: Using C, as row 1.

Row 8: Using A, k to end.

Row 9: Using A, as row 1.

Using A, cast off loosely in rib.

TO MAKE UP

Join side and armhole border seams. Press lightly following instructions on ball band.

A	45	(47.5,	50.5,	53,	56)	cm
	17¾	(18¾,	19¾,	20¾,	22)	in
B	19	(20,	21,	22,	23)	cm
	7½	(7¾,	8¼,	8¾,	9)	in
C	42					cm
	16½					in
D	5					cm
	2					in
E	28	(28,	29,	30,	31)	cm
	11	(11,	11½,	12,	12¼)	in
F	3	(3.5,	3.5,	3.5,	3.5)	cm
	1¼	(1½,	1½,	1½,	1½)	in
G	16.5	(17.5,	18.5,	19.5,	20.5)	cm
	6½	(7,	7¼,	7¾,	8)	in

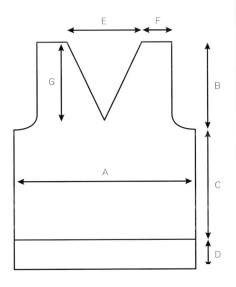

Claudette Colbert

Finished with a scattering of embroidered flowers, this long-sleeved, round-necked cardigan has puffed sleeves with turned-back cuffs. It is worked in textured basketweave stitch with double-rib welts. The neckband and borders are edged with a contrast yarn.

MEASUREMENTS

To fit bust:
76 (81, 86, 91, 97, 102)cm
30 (32, 34, 36, 38, 40)in

Actual measurements:
88 (92, 98, 106, 112, 116)cm

Length to shoulders:
56cm

Sleeve seam (excluding cuff):
44cm

See schematic for full measurements.

MATERIALS

Rowan Pure Wool DK (50g balls)
  6 (6, 6, 7, 7, 7) balls in in main colour A
  1 ball each of same in contrast colours B and C
A pair each of 3.25mm (UK 10) and 4mm (UK 8) knitting needles
4.00mm (UK 8) crochet hook
8 buttons

TENSION

22 sts and 30 rows to 10cm over patt using 4mm needles.

BACK

Using 4mm needles and A, cast on 84 (88, 94, 100, 106, 110) sts.
Work in patt as folls:
Row 1 (RS): Sl 1, k0 (1, 0, 0, 2, 0), p3 (4, 0, 3, 4, 0), *k4, p4; rep from * to last 8 (2, 5, 8, 3, 5) sts, k4 (2, 5, 4, 3, 5), p3 (0, 0, 3, 0, 0), k1(0, 0, 1, 0, 0).
Row 2 (WS): Sl 1, k3 (0, 0, 3, 0, 0), p4 (1, 4, 4, 2, 4), *k4, p4; rep from * to last 4 (6, 1, 4, 7, 1) sts, k4 (4, 1, 4, 4, 1), p0 (1, 0, 0, 2, 0), k0 (1, 0, 0, 1, 0).
Rows 3-6: Rep rows 1 and 2 twice.
Row 7: Sl 1, p0 (1, 0, 0, 2, 0), k3 (4, 0, 3, 4, 0), *p4, k4; rep from * to last 8 (2, 5, 8, 3, 5) sts, p4 (1, 4, 4, 2, 4), k4 (1, 1, 4, 1, 1).
Row 8: Sl 1, p3 (0, 0, 3, 0, 0), k4 (1, 4, 4, 2, 4), *p4, k4; rep from * to last 4 (6, 1, 4, 7, 1) sts, p3 (4, 0, 3, 4, 0), k1 (2, 1, 1, 3, 1).
Rows 9-12: Rep rows 7 and 8 twice.
These 12 rows form the patt.
Continuing in patt, work 12 rows.
Keeping patt correct, dec 1 st at each end of next and every foll alt row until 68 (72, 78, 84, 90, 94) sts remain, ending with a WS row.
Work 8 rows straight.
Keeping patt correct, inc 1 st each end of next and every foll alt row until there are 84 (88, 94, 100, 106, 110) sts.
Work straight until back measures 38 (37, 37, 37, 36, 36)cm from cast-on edge, ending with a WS row.

Shape armholes

Cast off 5 sts at beg of next 2 rows.
74 (78, 84, 90, 96, 100) sts
Keeping patt correct, dec 1 st at each end on next 5 (7, 9, 12, 13, 15) rows.
64 (64, 66, 66, 70, 70) sts.
Work straight until armholes measure 18 (19, 19, 19, 20, 20)cm from beg of shaping, ending with a WS row.
Cast off in patt.

LEFT FRONT

Using 4mm needles and A, cast on 6 (8, 11, 14, 17, 19) sts.
Work in patt as folls:
Row 1 (RS): Sl 1, k0 (1, 0, 0, 2, 0), p3 (4, 0, 3, 4, 0), [k4, p4] 0 (0, 1, 1, 1, 2) times, k2.
Row 2 (WS): Sl 1, p1, [k4, p4] 0 (0, 1, 1, 1, 2) times, k4 (4, 1, 4, 4, 1), p0 (1, 0, 0, 2, 0), k0 (1, 0, 0, 1, 0).
Row 3: Sl 1, k0 (1, 0, 0, 2, 0), p3 (4, 0, 3, 4, 0), [k4, p4] 0 (0, 1, 1, 1, 2) times, k2, cast on 4 sts. 10 (12, 15, 18, 21, 23) sts
Row 4: K2, p4, [k4, p4] 0 (0, 1, 1, 1, 2) times, k4 (4, 1, 4, 4, 1), p0 (1, 0, 0, 2, 0), k0 (1, 0, 0, 1, 0).
Row 5: Sl 1, k0 (1, 0, 0, 2, 0), p3 (4, 0, 3, 4, 0), [k4, p4] 0 (0, 1, 1, 1, 2) times, k4, p2, cast on 4 sts. 14 (16,19, 22, 25, 27) sts
Row 6: K1, p1, [k4, p4] 1 (1, 2, 2, 2, 3) times, k4 (4, 1, 4, 4, 1), p0 (1, 0, 0, 2, 0), k0 (1, 0, 0, 1, 0).

Claudette Colbert

Row 7: Sl 1, p0 (1, 0, 0, 2, 0), k3 (4, 0, 3, 4, 0), [p4, k4] 1 (1, 2, 2, 2, 3) times, p2, cast on 4 sts. 18 (20, 23, 26, 29, 31) sts.

Row 8: K1, p1, k4, [p4, k4] 1 (1, 2, 2, 2, 3) times, p3 (4, 0, 3, 4, 0), k1 (2, 1, 1, 3, 1).

Row 9: Sl 1, p0 (1, 0, 0, 2, 0), k3 (4, 0, 3, 4, 0), [p4, k4] 1 (1, 2, 2, 2, 3) times, p4, k2, cast on 4 sts. 22 (24, 27, 30, 33, 35) sts

Row 10: K2, [p4, k4] 2 (2, 3, 3, 3, 4) times, p3 (4, 0, 3, 4, 0), k1 (2, 1, 1, 3, 1).

Row 11: Sl 1, p0 (1, 0, 0, 2, 0), k3 (4, 0, 3, 4, 0), [p4, k4] 2 (2, 3, 3, 3, 4) times, p2, cast on 2 sts. 24 (26, 29, 32, 35, 37) sts

Row 12: K4, [p4, k4] 2 (2, 3, 3, 3, 4) times, p3 (4, 0, 3, 4, 0), k1 (2, 1, 1, 3, 1).

Continuing in patt as set, work 2 rows casting on 2 sts at end of next row, working cast-on sts in patt. 26 (28, 31, 34, 37, 39) sts

Work 2 rows inc once at end of next row. 27 (29, 32, 35, 38, 40) sts

Work 2 rows inc once at end of next row and at same edge of foll row. 29 (31, 34, 37, 40, 42) sts

Work 6 rows inc once at end of next and every alt row. 32 (34, 37, 40, 43, 45) sts

Patt 10 rows, dec 1 st at beg of next and every foll alt row **at the same time** inc 1 st at end of next and every foll alt row. 32 (34, 37, 40, 43, 45) sts

Work 2 rows, dec 1 st at beg of next row **at the same time** inc 1 st at end of next and at same edge of foll row. 33 (35, 38, 41, 44, 46) sts

Work 4 rows dec 1 st at beg of next and foll alt row **at the same time** inc 1 st at end of next and foll alt row. 33 (35, 38, 41, 44, 46) sts

Work 8 rows inc 1 st at end of next row. 34 (36, 39, 42, 45, 47) sts

Inc 1 st at beg of next and every foll alt row to 42 (44, 47, 50, 53, 55) sts.

Work straight until front measures same as back to beg of armhole shaping, ending with a WS row.

Shape armholes

Next row: Cast off 5 sts, patt to last st, k1. 37 (39, 42, 45, 48, 50) sts

Next row: Sl 1, patt to last st, k1.

****Work 5 (7, 9, 12, 13, 15) rows dec 1 st at armhole edge on every row. 32 (32, 33, 33, 35, 35) sts

Work straight until armhole measures 10 (11, 11, 11, 13, 13)cm from beg of shaping, ending with a WS row.

Shape neck

Dec 1 st at neck edge on next 14 rows. 18 (18, 19, 19, 21, 21) sts

Work straight until armhole measures same as back to shoulder.

Cast off in patt.****

RIGHT FRONT

Using 4mm needles and A, cast on 6 (8, 11, 14, 17, 19) sts.

Work in patt as folls:

Row 1 (RS): K2, [p4, k4] 0 (0, 1, 1, 1, 2) times, p3 (4, 0, 3, 4, 0), k1 (2, 1, 1, 3, 1).

Row 2 (WS): Sl 1, p0 (1, 0, 0, 2, 0), k3 (4, 0, 3, 4, 0), [p4, k4] 0 (0, 1, 1, 1, 2) times, p2, cast on 4 sts. 10 (12, 15, 18, 21, 23) sts

Row 3: K1, p1, k4, [p4, k4] 0 (0, 1, 1, 1, 2) times, p3 (4, 0, 3, 4, 0), k1 (2, 1, 1, 3, 1).

Row 4: Sl 1, p0 (1, 0, 0, 2, 0), k3 (4, 0, 3, 4, 0), [p4, k4] 0 (0, 1, 1, 1, 2) times, p4, k2, cast on 4 sts. 14 (16, 19, 22, 25, 27) sts

Row 5: K2, [p4, k4] 1 (1, 2, 2, 2, 3) times, p3 (4, 0, 3, 4, 0), k1 (2, 1, 1, 3, 1).

Row 6: Sl 1, p0 (1, 0, 0, 2, 0), k3 (4, 0, 3, 4, 0), [p4, k4] 1 (1, 2, 2, 2, 3) times, p2, cast on 4 sts. 18 (20, 23, 26, 29, 31) sts

Row 7: K2, p4, [k4, p4] 1 (1, 2, 2, 2, 3) times, k4 (4, 1, 4, 4, 1), p0 (1, 0, 0, 2, 0), k0 (1, 0, 0, 1, 0).

Row 8: Sl 1, k0 (1, 0, 0, 2, 0), p3 (4, 0, 3, 4, 0), [k4, p4] 1 (1, 2, 2, 2, 3) times, k4, p2, cast on 4 sts. 22 (24, 27, 30, 33, 35) sts

Row 9: K1, p1 [k4, p4] 2 (2, 3, 3, 3, 4) times, k4 (4, 1, 4, 4,1), p0 (1, 0, 0, 2, 0), k0 (1, 0, 0, 1, 0).

Row 10: Sl 1, k0 (1, 0, 0, 2, 0), p3 (4, 0, 3, 4, 0), [k4, p4] 2 (2, 3, 3, 3, 4) times, k2, cast on 2 sts. 24 (26, 29, 32, 35, 37) sts

Row 11: K1, p3, [k4, p4] 2 (2, 3, 3, 3, 4) times, k4 (4, 1, 4, 4,1), p0 (1, 0, 0, 2, 0), k0 (1, 0, 0, 1, 0).

Row 12: Sl 1, k0 (1, 0, 0, 2, 0), p3 (4, 0, 3, 4, 0), [k4, p4] 2 (2, 3, 3, 3, 4) times, k4, cast on 2 sts. 26 (28, 31, 34, 37, 39) sts

Continuing in patt as set, work 4 rows inc once at beg of 3rd row. 27 (29, 32, 35, 38, 40) sts

Work 2 rows inc 1 st at beg of next row and at the same edge of foll row. 29 (31, 34, 37, 40, 42) sts

Work 6 rows inc once at beg of next and every alt row. 32 (34, 37, 40, 43, 45) sts

Patt 10 rows inc 1 st at beg of next and every foll alt row **at the same time** dec 1 st at end of next and every foll alt row. 32 (34, 37, 40, 43, 45) sts

Work 2 rows inc 1 st at beg of next row and at same edge of foll row **at the same time** dec 1 st at end of next row. 33 (35, 38, 41, 44, 46) sts

Work 4 rows inc 1 st at beg of next and foll alt row **at the same time** dec 1 st at end of next and foll alt row. 33 (35, 38, 41, 44, 46) sts

Work 8 rows inc 1 st at beg of next row. 34 (36, 39, 42, 45, 47) sts

Work 16 rows inc 1 st at end of next and every foll alt row. 42 (44, 47, 50, 53, 55) sts

Work straight until front measures same as back to beg of armhole shaping, ending with a RS row.

Shape armholes

Next row: Cast off 5 sts, patt to last st, k1.

Now complete to match left front from ** to **.

SLEEVES

Using 3.25mm needles and A, cast on 44 (44, 44, 44, 48, 48) sts.

Rib row 1 (RS): Sl 1, k2, *p2, k2; rep from * to last st, k1.

Rib row 2 (WS): Sl 1, *p2, k2; rep from * to last 3 sts, p2, k1.

Rep these 2 rows 15 times more, inc 1 st at each end of last row. 46 (46, 46, 46, 50, 50) sts

Change to 4mm needles.

Work in patt as folls:
Row 1: Sl 1, p0 (0, 0, 0, 2, 2), *k4, p4;
rep from * to last 5 (5, 5, 5, 7, 7) sts, k4,
p0 (0, 0, 0, 2, 2), k1.
Row 2: Sl 1, k0 (0, 0, 0, 2, 2), p4, *k4, p4;
rep from * to last 1 (1, 1, 1, 3, 3) sts,
k1 (1, 1, 1, 3, 3).
Rows 3-6: Rep rows 1 and 2 twice.
Row 7: Sl 1, k0 (0, 0, 0, 2, 2), *p4, k4;
rep from * to last 5 (5, 5, 5, 7, 7) sts, p4,
k1 (1, 1, 1, 3, 3).
Row 8: Sl 1, p0 (0, 0, 0, 2, 2), k4, *p4, k4;
rep from * to last 1 (1, 1, 1, 3, 3) sts,
p0 (0, 0, 0, 2, 2), k1.
Rows 9-12: Rep rows 7 and 8 twice.
These 12 rows form the patt.
Continue in patt, inc and working into patt
1 st at each end of next and every foll 8th
(12th, 12th, 12th, 12th, 10th) rows to
70 (58, 58, 56, 62, 64) sts, then every
foll 4th row to 78 (80, 80, 84, 84, 86) sts
Work straight until sleeve measures 50cm
from cast-on edge, ending with a WS row.

Shape top
Keeping patt correct, dec 1 st at each end of
next and every foll 4th row until 62 (62, 62,
70, 66, 70) sts remain.
Dec 1 st at beg of next 6 (6, 6, 14, 10, 14)
rows. 56 sts
Cast off in patt.

TO MAKE UP
Using B, embroider flowers in lazy daisy
stitch (see page 91), then using straight
stitch and C, embroider stems as illustrated.
Join shoulder seams. Sew in sleeves,
pleating to fit at top.

Join side and sleeve seams.

Edging: With RS facing and using 4mm
crochet hook, join on C at lower edge of
right-hand side seam and work 2 rows of
double crochet up right front, round back
neck, down left front, and along lower edge,
working 8 buttonloops evenly spaced up
right front edge by working 2 ch and
missing 2 dc for each loop.

A	44	(46,	49,	53,	56,	58) cm
	17½	(18,	19¼,	21,	22,	23) in
B	18	(19,	19,	19,	20,	20) cm
	7	(7½,	7½,	7½,	7¾,	7¾) in
C	30	(29,	29,	29,	28,	28) cm
	12	(11½,	11½,	11½,	11,	11) in
D	8	cm				
	3¼	in				
E	9.5	(9.5,	10,	10,	11,	11) cm
	3¾	(3¾,	4,	4,	4¼,	4¼) in
F	15	cm				
	6	in				
G	22	(23,	25,	26,	28,	29) cm
	8¾	(9,	9¾,	10¼,	11,	11½) in
H	36	(38,	41,	44,	47,	49) cm
	14¼	(15,	16,	17½,	18½,	19¼) in
I	41	(42,	42,	44,	44,	45) cm
	16	(16½,	16½,	17½,	17½,	17¾) in
J	40	cm				
	15¾	in				
K	10	cm				
	4	in				
L	24	(24,	24,	24,	26,	26) cm
	9½	(9½,	9½,	9½,	10¼,	10¼) in
M	8	cm				
	3¼	in				

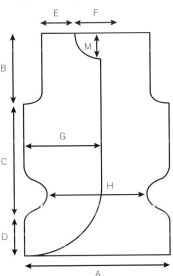

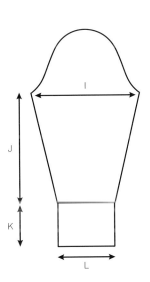

Claudette Colbert
1903 – 1996

Claudette Colbert, as her name
suggests, was born in Paris. She
was educated in New York where
her parents moved when she was
six, and became a stenographer,
but she yearned to be an actress.
She achieved this ambition on
the New York stage, but was
soon contracted to Paramount
where she made innumerable
movies. It was on loan from them
to Columbia that she made one
of the best films of her career, *It
Happened One Night* (1934) with
Clark Gable. Both won Oscars,
much to her amazement, since she
didn't relish her role as a runaway
heiress plagued by a reporter, but
the innovative treatment of this
comedy established Colbert as a
fine comedienne with a dry sense
of humour and superb timing.

With her versatile range, Cecil
B. DeMille chose her to play the
title role of *Cleopatra* (1934) – an
epic on a grand scale which
has Colbert scantily, but richly,
clad and bejewelled slithering
across super-shiny palace floors,
scheming, pouting and using all
her womanly wiles as befits
Egypt's notorious queen. In the
1940s she was one of Hollywood's
highest paid stars.

Movie-goers loved her – she
was confident and vulnerable at
the same time, convincing with
ease in tear jerkers or as a wicked
femme fatale. She had a strange
feline face, rounded cheeks, deep
expressive eyes and an endearing
smile. She was a superb clothes
horse, so it was not surprising
that even as a superstar she
occasionally posed for fashion stills.

Claudette Colbert enjoyed a
highly successful film career and
returned to the London stage at
the age of 82, starring in *Aren't
We All?* with Rex Harrison, still
able to captivate her audience.

Gary Cooper

Here is a classic double-knit men's sweater with set-in sleeves and a round neck. Made in stocking stitch, it has a simple Fair Isle design across the yoke and sleeves, worked from a chart. The yarn is machine washable for easy care.

MEASUREMENTS

To fit chest:
91 (97, 102, 107, 112)cm
36 (38, 40, 42, 44)in

Actual measurements:
101 (106, 112, 116, 121)cm

Length to shoulders:
64 (65, 66, 68, 69)cm

Sleeve seam:
48 (48, 50, 50, 51)cm

See schematic for full measurements.

MATERIALS

Rowan Pure Wool DK (50g balls)
9 (10, 10, 11, 12) balls in main colour A
2 (2, 2, 3, 3) balls in contrast colour B
1 (1, 1, 1, 2) balls in contrast colour C
A pair each of 3.25mm (UK 10), 4mm (UK 8) and 4.5mm (UK 7) knitting needles
Stitch holders

TENSION

22 sts and 30 rows to 10cm over st st using 4mm needles.

FRONT

**Using 3.25mm needles and A, cast on 101 (107,113,117,123) sts
Rib row 1 (RS): K1, *p1, k1; rep from * to end.
Rib row 2 (WS): P1, *k1, p1; rep from * to end.
Rep these 2 rows until piece measures 7.5cm, ending with rib row 1.
Inc row (WS): Rib 6 (8, 8, 10, 8), *M1, rib 10 (10, 11, 11, 12); rep from * to last 5 (9, 6, 8, 7) sts, M1, rib 5 (9, 6, 8, 7). 111 (117, 123, 127, 133) sts
Change to 4mm needles.
Starting with a RS knit row, work in st st until front measures 41 (41, 42, 42, 43)cm from cast-on edge, ending with a WS row.

Shape armholes

Cast off 3 (3, 4, 4, 4) sts at beg of next 2 rows. 105 (111, 115, 119, 125) sts
Dec 1 st at each end of next and foll alt row. 101 (107, 111, 115, 121) sts
P 1 row.
Change to 4.5mm needles and commence chart as folls:
Working the two-colour Fair Isle technique, reading odd numbered (k) rows from right to left and even numbered (p) rows from left to right, work in patt from Front and Back Chart, decreasing as indicated, until row 34 has been completed. 91 (93, 95, 97, 103) sts
Change to 4mm needles.
Continuing in A only, work 2 rows in st st.**

Shape neck

Next row: K37 (37, 38, 38, 41), turn and leave remaining sts on a stitch holder.
Dec 1 st at neck edge on next and every foll alt row until 24 (24, 25, 25, 27) sts remain.
Work straight until the armhole measures 23 (24, 24, 25, 26)cm from beg of shaping, ending at the armhole edge.

Shape shoulder

Cast off 8 (8, 8, 8, 9) sts at beg of next and foll alt row. 8 (8, 9, 9, 9) sts
Work 1 row. Cast off.
Return to remaining sts.
With RS facing, leaving first 17 (19, 19, 21, 21) sts on holder, join A to next st and k to end of row. 37 (37, 38, 38, 41) sts
Now complete to match first side of neck.

BACK

Work as given for Front from ** to **.
Continue straight in st st until back measures the same length as front to beg of shoulder shaping, ending with a WS row.

Shape shoulders

Cast off 8 (8, 8, 8, 9) sts at beg of next 4 rows, and 8 (8, 9, 9, 9) sts at beg of foll 2 rows.
Cut yarn and leave remaining 43 (45, 45, 47, 49) sts on a stitch holder.

SLEEVES

Using 3.25mm needles and A, cast on 45 (47, 49, 51, 53) sts

Gary Cooper

Work the 2 rib rows as set for front for 7.5cm, ending with rib row 1.

Inc row (WS): Rib 3 (4, 2, 3, 4), *M1, rib 3; rep from * to last 3 (4, 2, 3, 4) sts, M1, rib to end. 59 (61, 65, 67, 69) sts

Change to 4mm needles.

Starting with a RS knit row, work in st st increasing 1 st at each end of 9th and every foll 6th row to 95 (97, 101, 103, 105) sts. Work straight until sleeve measures 48 (48, 50, 50, 51)cm from cast-on edge, ending with a WS row.

Shape top

Cast off 3 (3, 4, 4, 4) sts at beg of next 2 rows. 89 (91, 93, 95, 97) sts

Dec 1 st at each end of next and foll alt row. 85 (87, 89, 91, 93) sts

P 1 row.

Change to 4.5mm needles.

Work in patt from Sleeve Chart, decreasing as indicated, until row 34 has been completed. 49 (53, 55, 57, 59) sts

Change to 4mm needles.

Working in A only and continuing in st st, cast off 2 sts at beg of next 2 rows and 5 sts at beg of foll 4 rows. 25 (29, 31, 33, 35) sts

Cast off.

NECKBAND

Join right shoulder seam.

With RS facing, join A to neck at left shoulder and using 3.25mm needles, pick up and k22 (24, 25, 28, 30) sts down left side of front neck, k the front neck sts from holder, pick up and k22 (24, 25, 28, 30) sts up right side of front neck, then increasing 1 st at centre k the back neck sts from holder. 105 (113, 115, 125, 131) sts

Beg with WS rib row 2, work 6 rows in rib as set for front.

Cast off loosely in rib.

TO MAKE UP

Join left shoulder and neckband seam. Set in the sleeves, then join side and sleeve seams. Press lightly foll instructions on ball band.

A (Main colour)
B (Contrast colour)
C (Contrast colour)

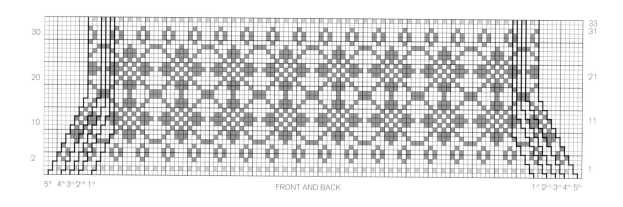

FRONT AND BACK

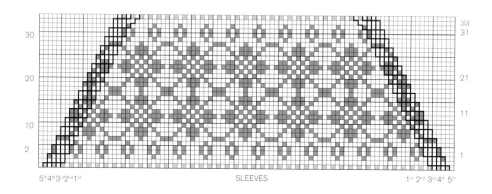

SLEEVES

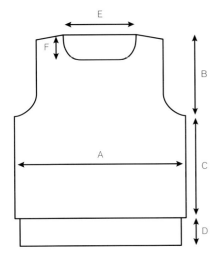

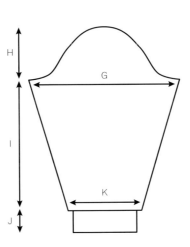

A	51	(53.5,	56,	58.5,	61)	cm
	20	(21,	22,	23,	24)	in
B	23	(24,	24,	25,	26)	cm
	9	(9½,	9½,	9¾,	10)	in
C	33.5	(33.5,	34.5,	35.5,	35.5)	cm
	13¼	(13¼,	13½,	13¾,	13¾,	in
D	7.5	cm				
	3	in				
E	19	(20,	20,	21,	22)	cm
	7½	(7¾,	7¾,	8¼,	8¾)	in
F	8	(9,	9,	10,	10)	cm
	3¼	(3½,	3½,	4,	4)	in

G	43	(44,	46,	47,	48)	cm
	17	(17½,	18,	18½,	19)	in
H	17	(18,	18,	19,	20)	cm
	6¾	(7,	7,	7½,	7¾)	in
I	40.5	(40.5,	42.5,	42.5	43.5)	cm
	16	(16,	16½,	16½,	17¼)	in
J	7.5	cm				
	3	in				
K	23	(24,	24,	25,	25)	cm
	9	(9½,	9½,	9¾,	9¾)	in

Gary Cooper
1901 – 1961

Just as James Dean emerged as a new kind of hero in the 1950s, so did Gary Cooper in the 1930s. His career spanned 35 years and he was undoubtedly one of the greatest film stars Hollywood had ever known. He was much admired by his peers who were unanimously of the opinion that the great secret of his acting was to appear not to be acting at all. He had a natural charm and extremely good looks, and exuded a powerful sexuality that won him millions of female fans. He was equally popular with men, who identified with his heroic qualities, virility and 'down to earth' attitudes.

Born in 1901 to British immigrants, Cooper originally intended to make a living as an artist, but unable to find a job, he became a film extra in Hollywood. He was snatched quickly from the crowd to play in *The Winning of Barbara Worth* (1926) ,which starred Vilma Bánky. Within a few years he was a major star, acting with many of Hollywood's most glamorous women – Lupe Vélez in *The Wolf Song* (1929), Marlene Dietrich in *Morocco* (1930), Joan Crawford in *Today We Live* (1933) and Grace Kelly in the classic western *High Noon* (1952).

Over the decades, his eternal classic looks and relaxed poses were much emulated by photographers for the glossy fashion magazines who demanded Gary Cooper look-alikes. But underneath his cool nonchalant exterior lay a workman who planned his roles with great care and precision. Years later, he remains a true megastar of the film industry.

Joan Crawford

This smart but feminine jumper has short puffed sleeves and a simple round neck. The welts are worked in double rib while the main fabric is in an attractive but simple variation of garter stitch with every row knitted – making for quick progress.

MEASUREMENTS

To fit bust:
76 (81, 86, 91, 97, 102)cm
30 (32, 34, 36, 38, 40)in

Actual measurements:
86 (91, 96, 100, 107, 112)cm

Length to shoulders:
54 (53, 53, 53, 52, 52)cm

Sleeve seam:
21cm

See schematic for full measurements.

MATERIALS

Rowan Pure Wool DK (50g balls)
    6 (7, 7, 7, 8, 8) balls
A pair each of 3.25mm (UK 10)
    and 4mm (UK 8) knitting needles
Stitch holders

TENSION

17 sts to 10cm over patt using
4mm needles.

BACK

**Using 3.25mm needles cast on
84 (88, 96, 100, 108, 112) sts
Rib row 1 (RS): Sl 1, k2, *p2, k2; rep from * to last st, k1.
Rib row 2 (WS): Sl 1, *p2, k2; rep from * to last 3 sts, p2, k1.
Rep these 2 rows 10 times more, then rib row 1 again.
Dec row (WS): Sl 1, p0 (2, 4, 6, 4, 6), *p2tog, p6(6,4,4,4,4), rep from * 9(9,13,13,15,15) times more, p2tog, p0 (2, 4, 6, 4, 6), k1. 73 (77, 81, 85, 91, 95) sts
Change to 4mm needles.
K 2 rows.
Continue in patt as follows:
Row 1 (RS): Sl 1, *K1B, k1; rep from * to end.
Row 2 (WS): Sl 1, k to end.
Row 3: Sl 1, k1, *K1B, k1; rep from * to last st, k1.
Row 4: Sl 1, k to end.
These 4 rows form the patt.
Continue in patt until work measures 36 (34, 34, 34, 33, 33)cm from cast-on edge, ending with a WS row.

Shape armholes

Cast off 4 sts at beg of next 2 rows.
65 (69, 73, 77, 83, 87) sts
Dec 1 st at each end of every row until 51 (51, 55, 55, 57, 57) sts remain.**
Work straight until armholes measure 18 (19, 19, 19, 20, 20)cm from beg of shaping, ending with a WS row.

Shape shoulders

Next row: Cast off 12 (12, 14, 14, 15, 15) sts, patt across next 26 sts, cast off remaining 12 (12, 14, 14, 15, 15) sts.
Fasten off and leave remaining 27 sts on a stitch holder.

FRONT

Work as given for Back from ** to **.
Work straight until armholes measures 6 (8, 8, 8, 9, 9)cm from beg of shaping, ending with a WS row.

Shape neck

Next row (RS): Sl 1, patt 20 (20, 22, 22, 23, 23), turn and leave remaining sts on a stitch holder.
Working on the first set of sts only, continue as folls:
Next row (WS): Sl 1, patt to last st, k1.
***Dec 1 st at neck edge on next and every foll alt row until 12 (12, 14, 14, 15, 15) sts remain.
Work straight until front measures same as back to shoulders, ending at armhole edge.

Shape shoulder

Cast off.***
Return to remaining sts.
With RS facing, leaving first 9 sts on holder, join yarn to next st, k1, patt to last st, k1.
Next row (WS): Sl 1, patt to last st, k1.
Work as given for first side of neck from *** to ***.

SLEEVES

Using 3.25mm needles, cast on 56 (56, 60, 60, 64, 64) sts.
Work 13 rib rows as given for back.
Inc row (WS): Sl 1, p1 (1, 1, 1, 3, 3), *pfb, p4 (4, 8, 8, 8, 8); rep from * to last 4 (4, 4, 4, 6, 6) sts, pfb, p2 (2, 2, 2, 4, 4), k1. 67 (67, 67, 67, 71, 71) sts
Change to 4mm needles.
K 2 rows.
Continue in patt as given for back, increasing and working into patt 1 st at each end of 3rd and every foll 6th (4th, 4th, 4th, 4th, 4th) rows to 77 (83, 83, 83, 87, 87) sts.
Work straight until sleeve measures 21cm from cast-on edge, ending with a WS row.

Shape top

Dec 1 st at each end of next and every foll 4th row to 69 (75, 75, 75, 79, 79) sts.
Dec 1 st at beg of next 26 (32, 32, 32, 36, 36) rows. 43 sts
Next row: Sl 1, patt to last st, k1.
Cast off.

NECKBAND

Join right shoulder seam.
With RS facing, using 3.25mm needles, pick up and k30 sts evenly down left hand side of front neck, k across 9 sts from front neck holder as follows: k3, [M1, k3] twice, pick up and k30 sts evenly up right hand side of front neck, work across 27 sts from back neck holder as follows: k1, [M1, k5] 5 times, M1, k1. 104 sts
Beg with WS rib row 2, work 11 rows in rib.
Cast off loosely in rib.

TO MAKE UP

Join left shoulder and neckband seam. Join side and sleeve seams. Sew in sleeves, forming pleats at top of sleeve to fit. Fold back cuffs.

A	43	(45.5,	48,	50,	53.5,	56)	cm
	17	*(18,*	*19,*	*19½,*	*21,*	*22)*	*in*
B	18	(19,	19,	19,	20,	20)	cm
	7¼	*(7½,*	*7½,*	*7½,*	*7¾,*	*7¾)*	*in*
C	29	(27,	27,	27,	26,	26)	cm
	11½	*(10¾,*	*10¾,*	*10¾,*	*10¼,*	*10¼)*	*in*
D	7	cm					
	2¾	*in*					
E	16	cm					
	6¼	*in*					
F	12	(11,	11,	11,	11,	11)	cm
	4¾	*(4¼,*	*4¼,*	*4¼,*	*4¼,*	*4¼)*	*in*
G	30	(30,	32,	32,	33,	33)	cm
	12	*(12,*	*12½,*	*12½,*	*13,*	*13)*	*in*
H	45	(50,	50,	50,	51,	51)	cm
	17¾	*(19½,*	*19½,*	*19½,*	*20,*	*20)*	*in*
I	39	(39,	39,	39,	42,	42)	cm
	15½	*(15½,*	*15½,*	*15½,*	*16½,*	*16½)*	*in*
J	12	cm					
	4¾	*in*					
K	9	cm					
	3½	*in*					

Joan Crawford
1905 – 1977

Joan Crawford once said: 'I wouldn't copy anybody. If I can't be me I don't want to be anybody. I was born that way.' Certainly, this most durable of stars was not a copier or a follower of anybody or anything.

Born Lucille LeSueur on the wrong side of the tracks in San Antonio, Texas in 1905, she arrived in Hollywood aged 19. Work in silent pictures soon followed and in 1928 she played a flapper in *Our Dancing Daughters* and emerged a star. She made an easy transition into talkies, her most notable starring roles being in *The Women* (1939), *Mildred Pierce* (1945), and *Johnny Guitar* (1954). She was rarely away from films for long and continued to act until the 1970s.

Crawford perhaps survived because she adapted physically to changing fashions, without submerging her essential film personality one iota. She always remained a sufferer (whether at the bottom or the top of the heap), but a sufferer defiantly facing the future.

Her trademarks were sophistication and independence. Wide shoulders, padded sweaters, severe dresses, all suggested someone able to face anything life threw at her. These outfits suited women during and after World War II, perhaps because some of them were enjoying freedom and independence for the first time. Later, Joan's well-cut sweaters and dresses would be swathed in furs and draped with jewels – but her defiance and independence were still there, mesmerising whole new generations.

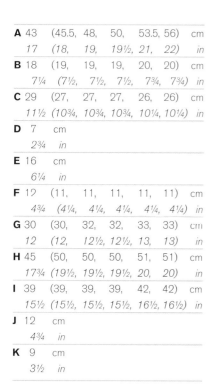

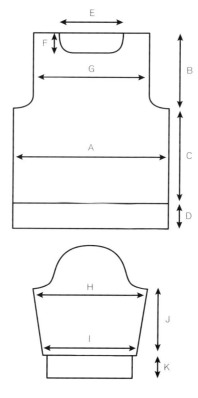

Peggy Cummins

The figure-hugging polo-necked sweater shown on page 33 is quick to knit in stocking stitch with double-rib detailing at the cuffs, hem and neckband. The set-in sleeves are given a feminine 1940s' look with the help of shoulder pads. For a neat roll-neck, the neckband is turned in and slipstitched.

MEASUREMENTS

To fit bust:
81 (86, 91, 97)cm
32 (34, 36, 38)in

Actual measurements:
88 (92, 98, 102)cm

Length to shoulders:
55 (56, 57, 58)cm

Sleeve seam:
44 (45, 45, 46)cm

See schematic for full measurements.

MATERIALS

Rowan Pure Wool Worsted
  (100g balls)
  5 (5, 5, 5) x 100g balls
A pair each of 3.75mm (UK 9) and
  4.5mm (UK 7) knitting needles
Stitch holders
Shoulder pads

TENSION

19 sts and 24 rows to 10cm over st st using 4.5mm needles.

BACK

Using 3.75mm needles, cast on
68 (72, 78, 82) sts.
Work 16 rows in [k2, p2] rib and inc 1 st at each end of last rib row. 70 (74, 80, 84) sts
Change to 4.5mm needles.
Beg with a RS knit row, work in st st and inc 1 st at each end of next and every foll 8th row to 84 (88, 94, 98) sts.
Work straight until back measures 27.5 (28.5, 28.5, 29.5)cm from cast-on edge, ending with a WS row.

Shape armholes

Cast off 3 sts at beg of next 2 rows.
78 (82, 88, 92) sts
Dec 1 st at each end of next 2 rows, then each end of every foll alt row until 68 (72, 76, 80) sts remain.
Work straight until back measures 55 (56, 57, 58)cm from cast-on edge, ending with a WS row.

Shape shoulders

Cast off 21 (23, 24, 26) sts at beg of next 2 rows.
Break yarn and leave remaining 26 (26, 28, 28) sts on a stitch holder.

FRONT

Work as given for Back until front measures 46 (47, 47, 48)cm from cast-on edge, ending with a WS row.

Shape neck

Next row (RS): K31 (33, 35, 37), turn and leave remaining sts on a stitch holder.
Working on these sts for first side of neck, dec 1 st at neck edge on every row until 23 (25, 27, 29) sts remain, then on every foll alt row until 21 (23, 24, 26) sts remain.
Work straight until front measures same as back to shoulder, ending with a WS row.
Cast off.
Return to remaining sts.
With RS facing, leaving first 6 sts on holder, join yarn and k to end.
Complete second side of neck to match first, reversing all shaping.

SLEEVES

Using 3.75mm needles, cast on 40 (40, 44, 44) sts.
Work 12 rows in [k2, p2] rib.
Change to 4.5mm needles.
Beg with a RS knit row, work in st st and inc 1 st at each end of next and every foll

Peggy Cummins
1925 – present day

Born in Prestatyn, North Wales, Peggy Cummins spent her childhood in Ireland. In 1938 she came to London to do radio shows and act, and here she was spotted by a 20th Century Fox talent scout. He saw her as the star of *Forever Amber* (1947), but Hollywood's Linda Darnell won the day, probably because the latter was more established and a bigger box-office pull.

Her first major Hollywood film *The Late George Apley* (1947) teamed her with such distinguished company as Ronald Colman, one of the great stars of Hollywood's Golden Age, and the sprightly character actress Mildred Natwick. In the same year, 1947, she starred opposite Victor Mature in *Moss Rose*, a Victorian melodrama in which she played a lively cockney music-hall floosie intent on getting her man and on the way becoming embroiled in murder and intrigue.

She returned to England to appear in *Escape* (1948) with Rex Harrison, returning briefly to Hollywood to star in the now respected cult B movie *Gun Crazy* (1950), a savage gangster film and forerunner of *Bonnie and Clyde*.

Thus ended her brief Hollywood career. Competition in Hollywood was tough, and quite a few Celtic beauties, such as Maureen O'Hara, Deborah Kerr and Greer Garson, were already firmly established there. Maybe Peggy was one too many. With her soft blonde hair and innocent green eyes she was nevertheless an engaging girl whom international success only just eluded. Ironically she is wearing one of the most sensual sweaters in the book: could it be that a potential sex symbol was always lurking underneath?

4th row to 50 (50, 54, 54) sts, then every foll 5th row to 76 (76, 80, 80) sts.
Work straight until sleeve measures 44 (45, 45, 46)cm from cast-on edge, ending with a WS row.
Shape top
Cast off 3 sts at beg of next 4 rows.
38 (38, 42, 42) sts
Dec 1 st at each end of every row until 36 (36, 40, 40) sts remain, then every foll alt row until 30 (30, 32, 32) sts remain.
Cast off 4 sts at beg of next 4 rows.
14 (14, 16, 16) sts
Cast off.

NECKBAND
Join right shoulder seam.
With RS facing, using 3.75mm needles, pick up and k20 (20, 23, 23) sts down left hand side of front neck, k6 sts from front neck holder, pick up and k20 (20, 23, 23) sts up right hand side of front neck, k26 (26, 28, 28) sts from back neck holder.
72 (72, 80, 80) sts
Work in [k2, p2] rib for 18cm.
Cast off in rib.

TO MAKE UP
Join left shoulder and neckband seam.
Fold sleeves in half lengthwise, then placing folds at top of sleeves to shoulder seams, sew in the sleeves.
Join side and sleeve seams. Sew in shoulder pads. Fold neckband in half to wrong side and slipstitch into place.

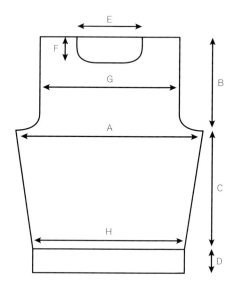
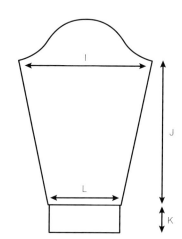

A	44	(46,	49,	51)	cm
	17½	(18,	19¼,	20)	in
B	27.5	(27.5,	28.5,	28.5)	cm
	11	(11,	11¼,	11¼)	in
C	21.5	(22.5,	22.5,	23.5)	cm
	8½	(8¾,	8¾,	9¼)	in
D	6	cm			
	2¼	in			
E	14	(14,	15,	15)	cm
	5½	(5½,	6,	6)	in
F	9	(9,	10,	10)	cm
	3½	(3½,	4,	4)	in
G	36	(38,	40,	42)	cm
	14	(15,	15¾,	16½)	in
H	37	(39,	42,	44)	cm
	14½	(15½,	16½,	17½)	in

I	40	(40,	42,	42)	cm
	15¾	(15¾,	16½,	16½)	in
J	39	(40,	40,	41)	cm
	15½	(15¾,	15¾,	16)	in
K	5	cm			
	2	in			
L	21	(21,	23,	23)	cm
	8¼	(8¼,	9,	9)	in

Errol Flynn

This man's V-necked sweater with set-in sleeves is worked in a simple variation of garter stitch using the K1B stitch (see main Abbreviations list on page 87). Because every row is knitted, the sweater soon grows despite its size. The single-rib neckband is worked on a circular needle to avoid a seam.

(see main Abbreviations list on page 87)

MEASUREMENTS

To fit chest:
92-97 (102-107, 112-117)cm
36-38 (40-42, 44-46)in

Actual measurements:
108 (117, 126)cm

Length to shoulders:
63 (65, 67)cm

Sleeve seam:
47 (48, 49)cm

See schematic for full measurements.

MATERIALS

Rowan Pure Wool 4ply (50g balls)
    12 (13, 14) balls
A pair each of 3mm (UK 11) and
    3.75mm (UK 9) knitting needles
A set of 3mm (UK 11) circular
    needles, 60cm (24in) long
Stitch holders
Safety pin
Stitch marker

TENSION

18 sts and 48 rows to 10cm
over patt using 3.75mm needles.

BACK

**Using 3mm needles, cast on 97 (105, 113) sts.
Rib row 1 (RS): K1, *p1, k1; rep from * to end.
Rib row 2 (WS): P1, *k1, p1; rep from * to end.
Rep these 2 rows for 5cm, ending with rib row 1.
Change to 3.75mm needles.
K 1 row.
Continue in patt as follows:
Row 1 (RS): K1, *K1B, k1; rep from * to end.
Row 2 (WS): K to end.
Row 3: K2, *K1B, k1; rep from * to last st, k1.
Row 4: K to end.
These 4 rows form the patt.
Continue in patt until work measures 41 (42, 43)cm from cast-on edge, ending with a WS row.
Shape armholes
Keeping patt correct, cast off 4 sts at beg of next 2 rows, then 2 sts at beg of foll 2 rows. 85 (93, 101) sts
Dec 1 st at each end of next and every foll alt row until 77 (83, 89) sts remain.**
Work straight until armholes measure 22 (23, 24)cm from beg of shaping, ending with a WS row.

Shape shoulders
Cast off 7 (8, 9) sts at beg of next 4 rows, then 8 (9, 10) sts at beg of foll 2 rows. Break yarn and leave remaining 33 sts on a stitch holder.

FRONT

Work as given for Back from ** to **.
Work straight until armholes measure 3 (4, 5)cm from beg of shaping, ending with a WS row.
Shape neck
Next row (RS): Patt 38 (41, 44) sts, turn and leave remaining sts on a stitch holder.
Next row (WS): K to end.
***Dec 1 st at neck edge on next and every foll 4th row until 22 (25, 28) sts remain.
Work straight until front measures same as back to shoulder, ending at armhole edge.
Shape shoulder
Cast off 7 (8, 9) sts at beg of next and foll alt row.
Work 1 row, then cast off.***
Return to remaining sts.
With RS facing, slip first st onto a safety-pin, rejoin yarn to next st and patt 2 rows.
Complete as given for first side of neck from *** to ***.

SLEEVES

Using 3mm needles, cast on 53 (55, 57) sts.
Work in rib as given for back for 8cm,
ending with rib row 1.
Change to 3.75mm needles.
K 1 row.
Continue in patt as given for back and
at the same time inc and work into patt
1 st at each end of 9th and every foll
12th row to 79 (83, 87) sts.
Work straight until sleeve measures
47 (48, 49)cm from cast-on edge, ending
with a WS row.

Shape top

Cast off 4 sts at beg of next 2 rows, then
2 sts at beg of foll 6 rows and 3 sts at beg
of foll 16 rows. 11 (15,19) sts
Cast off.

NECKBAND

Join shoulder seams.
With RS facing and using the circular
needle, patt across 33 sts from back neck
holder, pick up and k66 sts down left hand
side of front neck, k the centre st from
safety-pin, then pick up and k66 sts up
right hand side of front neck. 166 sts
Join in the round, placing a marker for beg
of round and continue as folls:
Round 1: [K1, p1] to within 1 st of centre
front st, slip 2 sts together knitwise, k1, pass
the 2 slip sts over the knit st, [p1, k1] to end.
Round 2: Rib to within 1 st of centre
front st, slip 2 sts together knitwise, k1,
pass the 2 slip sts over the knit st, rib to end.
Rep round 2 for 3cm.
Cast off in rib, decreasing at centre front
as before.

TO MAKE UP

Fold sleeves in half lengthwise, then
placing folds at top of sleeves to shoulder
seams, sew into place. Join side and
sleeve seams.

A	54	(58.5,	63)	cm
	21¼	(23,	24¾)	in
B	22	(23,	24)	cm
	8¾	(9,	9½,	in
C	36	(37,	38)	cm
	14	(14½,	15)	in
D	5			cm
	2			in
E	18			cm
	7			in
F	20			cm
	7¾			in
G	44	(46,	48)	cm
	17½	(18,	19)	in
H	5			cm
	2			in
I	39	(40,	41)	cm
	15½	(15¾,	16)	in
J	8			cm
	3¼			in
K	29.5	(30.5,	31.5)	cm
	11½	(12,	12½)	in

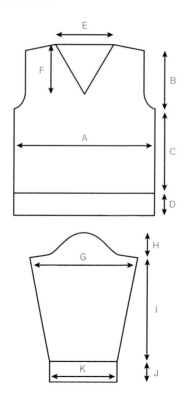

Errol Flynn
1909 – 1959

Errol Flynn's very name conjures
up the vitality and romance
unique to him. Extremely
handsome and virile, this hero's
youthful adventures made him a
suitable candidate for *Boys' Own
Annual*; by 24 he had prospected
for gold, hunted tropical birds
and smuggled diamonds.

His appearance as Fletcher
Christian in the early Australian
film *In the Wake of the Bounty* (1933)
prompted a move to England
and then to Hollywood, where
he soon landed a contract
with Warner Brothers. Here
he was teamed with another
newcomer, Olivia de Havilland,
in a series of successful and
exciting swashbucklers such as
Captain Blood (1935), *The Charge
of the Light Brigade* (1936) and *The
Adventures of Robin Hood* (1938).
*The Private Lives of Elizabeth and
Essex* (1939) with Bette Davis
was also a big success and the
public, press and Hollywood
adored him. His golden years
were 1935–1942.

His charming smile, assured
gallantry and animal magnetism
naturally attracted women on
a grand scale and although
he was married (three times),
Flynn's womanising and drinking
were legendary. But his romantic
escapades culminated in a
court case for statutory rape,
and although he was acquitted,
Flynn lost himself in fabled bouts
of drinking, and finally died of
a heart attack in Vancouver,
Canada, aged 50.

Apart from Douglas Fairbanks
Snr., no one smiled with such
charm, looked so dashing in
hose or breeches, or generally
swashed a buckle with such an
air as Errol Flynn.

Greta Garbo

MEASUREMENTS

To fit bust:
86 (91, 97)cm
34 (36, 38)in

Actual measurements:
96 (100, 106)cm

Length to shoulders:
75 (75, 76)cm

Sleeve seam:
42cm

*See schematic for full
measurements.*

MATERIALS

Rowan Tweed DK (50g balls)
    11 (12, 13) balls in main colour A
    1 ball in contrast colour B
A pair each of 3.25mm (UK 10)
    and 4mm (UK 8) knitting needles
Stitch holders
7 buttons

TENSION

21 sts and 30 rows to 10cm over
patt using 4mm needles.

Garbo's sweater shown on page 39 has set-in sleeves, a round neck and button-front opening. The sleeves are finished with button-up cuffs and there are two pockets on the front. It is knit in a textured hexagon and diamond pattern worked from the stitch chart. Pocket tops, cuffs, neckband and borders are all trimmed with contrast-colour stripes.

BACK

Using 3.25mm needles and A, cast on 101 (105, 111) sts.
Rib row 1 (RS): K1, *p1, k1; rep from * to end.
Rib row 2 (WS): P1, *k1, p1; rep from * to end.
Rep these 2 rows for 2.5cm, ending with a WS row.
Change to 4mm needles.
Following the chart, work the 20 row patt repeating the 9 st patt 11 times across the row and working the 1 (3, 6) edge sts as indicated, until back measures 57cm from cast-on edge, ending with a WS row.

Shape armholes

Keeping patt correct, cast off 3 (3, 4) sts at beg of next 2 rows, 2 (2, 3) sts at beg of next 2 rows, then 2 sts at beg of next 4 (4, 6) rows. 83 (87, 85) sts
Dec 1 st at beg of next 4 (6, 2) rows.
79 (81, 83) sts
Work straight until back measures 75 (75, 76)cm from cast-on edge, ending with a WS row.

Shape shoulders

Cast off 3 (4, 4) sts at beg of next 2 rows and 4 sts at beg of foll 4 rows.
57 (57, 59) sts

Shape neck

Next row (RS): Cast off 4 sts, patt until there are 20 (20, 21) sts on the needle, cast off 9 sts, patt to end.
Work on first set of sts as folls:
Next row: Cast off 4 sts, patt to end.
Next row: Cast off 6 sts, patt to end.
Rep these 2 rows once more.
Cast off remaining 4 (4, 5) sts.
Return to remaining sts.
With WS facing, rejoin yarn to remaining sts, cast off 6 sts, patt to end.
Next row: Cast off 4 sts, patt to end.
Next row: Cast off 6 sts, patt to end.
Cast off remaining 4 (4, 5) sts.

POCKET LININGS

MAKE 2
Using 4mm needles and A, cast on 28 sts.
Beg with a RS knit row, work st st for 8cm, ending with a WS row.
Break yarn and leave sts on a stitch holder.

FRONT

Work as given for back until front measures 11cm from cast-on edge, ending with a WS row.

Greta Garbo

Place pockets
Next row (RS): Patt 10 (12, 15) sts, slip next 28 sts onto stitch holder and in their place patt across sts of first pocket lining, patt next 25 sts, slip next 28 sts onto stitch holder and in their place patt across sts of second pocket lining, patt to end. Continue in patt until work measures 51cm from cast-on edge, ending with a WS row.

Divide for front opening
Next row (RS): Patt 47 (49, 52) sts, cast off next 7 sts, patt to end.
Work on first side of neck as folls:
Keeping patt correct, work straight until front measures same as back to beg of armhole shaping, ending at armhole edge.

Shape armhole
Cast off 3 (3, 4) sts at beg of next row, 2 (2, 3) sts at beg of foll alt row, then 2 sts at beg of foll 2 (2, 3) alt rows. 38 (40, 40) sts
Dec 1 st at armhole edge at beg of foll 2 (3, 2) alt rows. 36 (37, 38) sts
Work straight until the front measures 11 rows less than the back to beg of shoulder shaping, ending at the neck edge.

Shape neck
Cast off 3 sts at beg of next row, then 2 sts at beg of foll 3 alt rows. 27 (28, 29) sts
Dec 1 st at neck edge at beg of foll 2 alt rows, so ending at armhole edge. 25 (26, 27) sts

Shape shoulder
Next row: Cast off 3 (4, 4) sts, patt to end.
Next row: Work 2 sts tog, patt to end.
Next row: Cast off 4 sts, patt to end.
Next row: Work 2 sts tog, patt to end.
Cast off 4 sts at beg of next and foll 2 alt rows. 4 (4, 5) sts
Work 1 row.
Cast off.
Return to remaining sts.
With WS facing, join on A and patt to end.
Complete to match first side of neck, reversing all shaping.

RIGHT SLEEVE
First half of cuff: Using 3.25mm needles and A, cast on 28 (28, 31) sts.
P 2 rows, k 1 row, p 1 row, then k 2 rows.
Join in B.
Next row (RS): With B, *k1, sl 1 pwise; rep from * to last st, k1.
Next row (WS): With B, *k1, yf, sl 1 pwise, yb; rep from * to last st, k1.
With A, k 3 rows, p 1 row, then k 2 rows.
Next row: With B, *k1, sl 1 pwise; rep from * to last st, k1.
Next row: With B, *k1, yf, sl 1 pwise, yb; rep from * to last st, k1.
Break yarn B.
With A, k 3 rows, p 1 row, then k 1 row.
Break yarn and leave sts on a stitch holder.
Second half of cuff: Using 3.25mm needles and A, cast on 24 (24, 27) sts and work as given for first half of cuff but **do not break** yarn.
Next row (WS): K19 (19, 22) of second cuff, then holding the 5 remaining sts of second cuff in front of the first 5 sts of first cuff, k2tog working 1 st from each needle five times, k remaining 22 (22, 26) sts. 47 (47, 53) sts
Change to 4mm needles.
Work in patt from chart and inc and work into patt 1 st at each end of 5th and every foll 6th row to 81 (81, 67) sts, then **for 3rd size only** inc 1 st at each end of every foll 7th row to 85 sts.
Work straight until sleeve measures 47 (48, 49)cm from cast-on edge, ending with a WS row.

Shape top
Cast off 3 sts at beg of next 2 rows and 2 sts at beg of foll 8 (8, 12) rows.
Dec 1 st at beg of next 34 (34, 30) rows.
Cast off 2 sts at beg of next 2 rows and 3 sts at beg of foll 2 rows.
Cast off remaining 15 sts.

LEFT SLEEVE
Work as given for right sleeve **but** work second half of cuff first, break yarn, then work first half of cuff but do not break off yarn and continue as folls:
Join cuff sections as follows:
Next row (WS): K22 (22, 26) of section just worked, then holding the 5 remaining sts of this cuff in front of the first 5 sts of second piece of cuff, k2tog working 1 st from each needle five times, k remaining 19 (19, 22) sts. 47 (47, 53) sts
Complete as given for right sleeve.

NECKBAND
Join shoulder seams.
With RS facing, using 3.25mm needles and A, pick up and k26 sts up right hand side of front neck, 39 sts across back neck, then 26 sts down left hand side of front neck. 91 sts
**P 1 row and k 2 rows.
Next row (RS): With B, *k1, sl 1 pwise; rep from * to last st, k1.
Next row (WS): With B, * k1, yf, sl 1 pwise, yb; rep from * to last st, k1.
Break B.
With A, k 3 rows, p 1 row, k 1 row, then p 3 rows.
Beg with a RS knit row, work 10 rows in st st.
Cast off very loosely.
Fold band in half to WS and slipstitch into position.**

FRONT BANDS
BOTH ALIKE
With RS facing, using 3.25mm needles and A, pick up and k49 sts evenly along front neck opening and neckband edge.
Work as given for neckband from ** to **.
Lap right band over left and neatly slipstitch lower edges into position.

POCKET TOPS
With RS facing, slip 28 sts from holder onto a 3.25mm needle, join on A and cast on 1 st. 29 sts
Work band as neckband from ** to **.

CUFF EDGING

With RS of cuff facing, using 3.25mm needles and A, pick up and k12 sts along outer edge of cuff opening.
K 2 rows.
Cast off knitwise.

TO MAKE UP

Work a button loop at lower edge of each outer cuff edging, sew button to inner cuff edge to correspond with button loop.
Work 5 button loops on right front edge, the first at top of neckband, the next 3cm from lower edge of neck opening and the rest evenly spaced.
Sew on the buttons to correspond with button loops. Sew down pocket linings, then sew down side edges of pocket tops. Sew in sleeves. Join side and sleeve seams.

A (K on RS rows, p on WS rows) ☐
B (P on RS rows, k on WS rows) ■

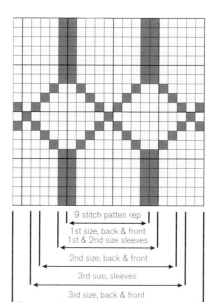

9 stitch patten rep
1st size, back & front
1st & 2nd size sleeves
2nd size, back & front
3rd size, sleeves
3rd size, back & front

A	48	(50,	53)	cm
	19	(19½,	21)	in
B	18	(18,	19)	cm
	7	(7,	7½)	in
C	54.5			cm
	21½			in
D	2.5			cm
	1			in
E	16			cm
	6¼			in
F	11	(11.5,	12)	cm
	4¼	(4½,	4¾)	in
G	10			cm
	4			in
H	14	(14,	15)	cm
	5½	(5½,	5¾)	in
I	3			cm
	1¼			in
J	38	(38,	40)	cm
	15	(15,	15¾)	in
K	37			cm
	14¼			in
L	5			cm
	2			in
M	22	(22,	25)	cm
	8¾	(8¾,	9¾)	in

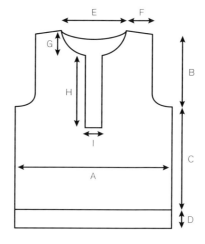

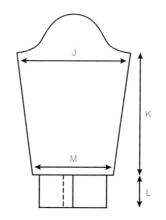

Greta Garbo
1905 – 1990

If Garbo had been asked to choose what she should wear to be photographed for this book, one feels it could have been this casual sweater and simple hat, a far cry from the clinging velvets and shimmering lamé she wore in her films.

Greta Louisa Gustafsson was born in Stockholm, Sweden, the daughter of a labourer. The young Garbo had worked in a department store, where her appearance in ads led to small film parts, and was studying at drama school when Mauritz Stiller, a notable Swedish director at the time, eventually Svengalied her off to Hollywood – but not to immediate fame. Although he was sacked from the silent movie *The Temptress* (1926), in which Garbo starred, she went from strength to strength. Her love scenes with Hollywood heartthrob John Gilbert were unforgettable for their steamy, sensuous passion.

Audiences were enraptured by her flawless appearance and simmering sensuality in several film classics in which she super-starred after a successful transition from silent films to the talkies. Her most memorable films were *Queen Christina* (1933), *Camille* (1936) and *Ninotchka* (1939). However, *Two-Faced Woman* (1941) failed at the box office and by chance or accident was Garbo's last-ever film. From the 1940s until her death in 1990, she lived a reclusive life in New York.

Garbo's presence is still felt today in fashion and beauty, and more than 80 years on, her style has never been matched.

Judy Garland

MEASUREMENTS

To fit bust:
81 (86, 91, 97)cm
32 (34, 36, 38)in

Actual measurements:
89 (94, 99, 104)cm

Length to shoulders:
47 (47, 48, 48)cm

Sleeve seam:
13cm

*See schematic for full
measurements.*

MATERIALS

Rowan Wool Cotton (50g balls)
   4 (4, 5, 5) balls
and
Orkney Angora St Magnus
   (50g balls) 2 (2, 3, 3) balls
A pair each of 4mm (UK 8) and
   4.5mm (UK 7) knitting needles
Stitch holders
Coloured tapestry yarn for
   embroidering flowers
Tapestry needle
8 buttons

TENSION

24 sts and 30 rows to 10cm over st
st using 4.5mm needles.

A cuddly angora blend and wool-cotton yarn combine to make this unusual stocking-stitch cardigan with short puffed sleeves shown on page 43. The button borders and sleeves are made in the angora yarn with the back and fronts knitted in the wool-cotton. A scattering of embroidered flowers worked in lazy daisy and satin stitch with French knots complete the picture.

BACK

Using 4mm needles and Rowan Wool Cotton, cast on 85 (89, 95, 99) sts.
Rib row 1 (RS): K1, *p1, k1; rep from * to end.
Rib row 2 (WS): P1, *k1, p1; rep from * to end.
Rep these 2 rows for 4cm, ending with rib row 1.
Inc row (WS): Rib 6 (4, 8, 6), *M1, rib 4; rep from * to last 7 (5, 7, 5) sts, M1, rib to end. 104 (110, 116, 122) sts
Change to 4.5mm needles.
Beg with a RS knit row, work in st st until back measures 27 (27, 28, 28)cm from cast-on edge, ending with a WS row.
Shape armholes
Cast off 6 sts at beg of next 2 rows.
92 (98, 104, 110) sts
Dec 1 st at each end of every row until 88 (88, 90, 90) sts remain.
Work straight until armholes measure 20 (20, 22, 22)cm from beg of shaping, ending with a WS row.

Shape shoulders
Cast off 16 sts at beg of next 4 rows.
Break yarn and leave remaining 24 (24, 26, 26) sts on a stitch holder.

LEFT FRONT

**Using 4mm needles and wool-cotton, cast on 43 (45, 47, 49) sts.
Work the 2 rib rows as for back for 4cm, ending with rib row 1.
Inc row (WS): Rib 6 (4, 4, 2), *M1, rib 4; rep from * to last 5 (5, 3, 3) sts, M1, rib to end. 52 (55, 58, 61) sts**
Change to 4.5mm needles.
Beg with a RS knit row, work in st st until left front measures same as back to armhole, ending with a WS row.
Shape armhole
Cast off 6 sts at beg of next row.
46 (49, 52, 55) sts
Work 1 row straight.
Dec 1 st at armhole edge on every row until 44 (44, 45, 45) sts remain.

Judy Garland

Work straight until armhole measures 11 (11, 13, 13)cm from beg of shaping, ending at front edge.

Shape neck
Cast off 6 sts at beg of next row.
Dec 1 st at neck edge on next and every foll alt row until 32 sts remain.
Work straight until front measures same as back to shoulder, ending at armhole edge.

Shape shoulder
Cast off 16 sts at beg of next row.
Work 1 row.
Cast off.

RIGHT FRONT
Work as left front from ** to **.
Change to 4.5mm needles.
Beg with a RS knit row, work in st st until right front measures same as back to armhole, ending with a **RS** row.
Complete as for left front, reversing all shaping.

SLEEVES
Using 4mm needles and angora, cast on 49 (49, 51, 51) sts.
Work the 2 rib rows for 3cm, ending rib row 1.
Inc row (WS): Rib 4 (4, 2, 2), *M1, rib 2; rep from * to last 3 sts, M1, rib to end.
71 (71, 75, 75) sts
Change to 4.5mm needles.
Beg with a RS knit row, work in st st until sleeve measures 13cm from cast-on edge, ending with a WS row.

Shape top
Cast off 6 sts at beg of next 2 rows.
59 (59, 63, 63) sts
Dec 1 st at beg of every row until 51 sts remain.
Work straight until sleeve measures 25 (25, 27, 27)cm from cast-on edge, ending with a WS row.
Cast off.

NECKBAND
Join shoulder seams.
With RS facing, using 4mm needles and angora, pick up and k23 sts up right hand front neck, k across 24 (24, 26, 26) sts from back neck holder, pick up and k24 sts down left hand front neck.
71 (71, 73, 73) sts
Beg with WS rib row 2, work 5 rows in rib.
Cast off in rib.

BUTTON BORDER
Using 4mm needles and angora, cast on 7 sts.
Rib row 1 (RS): K2, *p1, k1; rep from * to last st, k1.
Rib row 2 (WS): K1, *p1, k1; rep from * to end.
Rep these 2 rows until border, slightly stretched, fits up front to top of neckband. Sew on the border, then mark positions for 8 buttons, the first one 1.5cm from cast-on edge, the top one 1.5cm from cast-off edge and the others spaced evenly in between.

BUTTONHOLE BORDER
Work as given for button border, working buttonholes to correspond with markers as follows:
Buttonhole row (RS): K2, p1, yo, p2tog, k2.

TO MAKE UP
Sew on buttonhole border. Join side and sleeve seams. Sew in sleeves, forming gathers at top of sleeve to fit. Sew on buttons.
Using lazy daisy stitch for the leaves and satin stitch and French knots for the flowers (see page 91 for stitch instructions), embroider sprays of flowers as shown in illustrations, right.

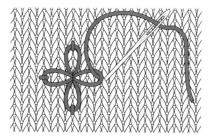

Lazy daisy stitch

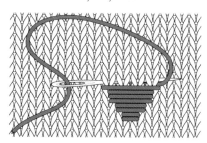

Satin stitch

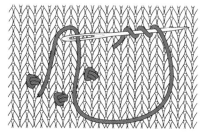

French knot

Judy Garland

A	43	(46,	48,	51)	cm
	17	(18,	19,	20)	in
B	20	(20,	22,	22)	cm
	7¾	(7¾,	8¾,	8¾)	in
C	23	(23,	24,	24)	cm
	9	(9,	9½,	9½)	in
D	4				cm
	1½				in
E	13				cm
	5¼				in
F	10	(10,	11,	11)	cm
	4	(4,	4¼,	4¼)	in
G	9				cm
	3½				in
H	21.5	(23,	24,	25.5)	cm
	8½	(9,	9½,	10)	in

I	30	(30,	31,	31)	cm
	12	(12,	12¼,	12¼)	in
J	12	(12,	14,	14)	cm
	4¾	(4¾,	5½,	5½)	in
K	10				cm
	4				in
L	3				cm
	1¼				in
M	21				cm
	8¼				in

Judy Garland
1922 – 1969

Judy Garland, born Frances Gumm, was destined to be a legend. Largely encouraged by her mother who was in vaudeville, Judy began her career at the age of three but from the beginning she was subjected to strict routine, prescribed diets and early calls. This probably accounted for her nervous disposition, but it was this very vulnerability that ignited the famous Judy Garland flame that held audiences spellbound all over the world. With her truly remarkable singing voice she could melt the hardest heart.

She made her first film in 1936 and in 1939 was cast as Dorothy in *The Wizard of Oz*. Garland made history. 'Over the Rainbow' became *her* song. Her follow-up films, including *Babes in Arms* (1939) and *Strike up the Band* (1940) both with Mickey Rooney, were also hits and her success was unquestionable. In *Meet Me in St Louis* (1944) directed by Vincent Minnelli, later to become her second husband, Judy beat all box office expectations, making the film the highest grossing movie musical up to that time. What could go wrong?

Sadly by the time she completed *A Star is Born* (1954), Garland had begun to burn herself out. Her increasing reliance on pills for zest took its toll, film offers dried up and in 1969 she died of an accidental overdose.

A perpetual Peter Pan with her innocent looks, on screen Judy Garland always looked flawless. She remains one of Hollywood's best-loved stars.

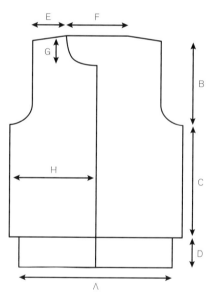

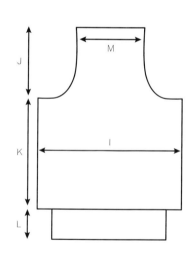

Cary Grant

The cricket-style sweater shown on page 47 has bold contrast stripes at the neck, cuffs and waist and is knitted in cotton. The welts are worked in double rib while the back, front and sleeves are knitted in panels of cable and stocking stitch. Choose cool white or cream and add your own contrast colours.

MEASUREMENTS

To fit chest:
86–91 (97–102, 107–112)cm
34 36 (38–40,42–44)in

Actual measurements:
112 (122, 132)cm

Length to shoulders:
69 (70, 71)cm

Sleeve seam:
55 (56, 57)cm

See schematic for full measurements.

MATERIALS

Debbie Bliss Cotton DK (50g balls)
    14 (15, 16) balls main colour A
    2 balls in contrast colour B
    1 ball in contrast colour C
A pair each of 3.25mm (UK 10) and
    4mm (UK 8) knitting needles
Cable needle
Stitch holders
Locking stitch marker

TENSION

20 sts and 26 rows to 10cm over
st st using 4mm needles.

SPECIAL ABBREVIATION

C8F (Cable 8 Front): Slip next
4 sts onto cable needle and hold
at front of work, k4, then k4 from
cable needle.

PATTERN NOTE

When using several colours in one row,
use a separate small ball of yarn for
each area of colour, and twist yarns
together on wrong side of work when
changing colour to avoid making a hole.

BACK

Using 3.25mm needles and A, cast on
108 (116, 124) sts.
Work 9cm in [k2, p2] rib, ending with a RS
row.
Inc row (WS): Rib 14 (9, 8), *M1,
rib 16 (14, 12); rep from * to last 14 (9, 8)
sts, M1, rib to end. 114 (124, 134) sts.
Change to 4mm needles.
Join and break colours as necessary.
Using B and beg with RS knit row, work
10 rows in st st.
Inc row (RS): Using A, k12 (14, 17),
*M1, k18 (19, 20); rep from * to last 12 (15,
17) sts, M1, k to end. 120 (130, 140) sts
Foundation row (WS): Using A, p14 (19,
24), [k2, p8] 9 times, k2, p14 (19, 24).
Continuing in A, work in patt as follows:
Row 1: K14 (19, 24), p2, [k8, p2] 9 times,
k14 (19, 24).
Row 2: P14 (19, 24), [k2, p8] 9 times, k2,
p14 (19, 24).
Row 3: K14 (19, 24), p2, [C8F, p2, k8, p2)
4 times, C8F, p2, k14 (19, 24).
Row 4: As row 2.
Row 5 to 10: Rep rows 1 and 2 three
times.

These 10 rows form patt.
Continue in patt until work measures
65 (66, 67)cm from cast-on edge, ending
with a WS row.
Set position for contrast stripes at neck as
folls:
Next row (RS): Patt 40 (45, 50)A, k40B,
with A patt to end.
Next row (WS): Patt 39 (44, 49)A, p42B,
with A patt to end.
Continue in this way, working 1 st less each
side in A and 2 more sts in B, for a further
4 rows.
Next row: Patt 35 (40, 45)A, k5B, k40C,
k5B, patt 35 (40, 45)A.
Next row: Patt 34 (39, 44)A, p5B, p42C,
p5B, patt 34 (39, 44)A.
Next row: Patt 34 (39, 44)A, k5B, k42C,
k5B, patt 34 (39, 44)A.
Next row: Patt 33 (38, 43)A, p5B, p44C,
p5B, patt 33 (38, 43)A.
Shape shoulders
Keeping colours and patt as set, cast off
21 (24, 27)sts at beg of next 2 rows, then
22 (24, 26)sts at beg of following 2 rows.
Break yarn and leave remaining 34 sts on
a holder.

FRONT

Work as given for back until front measures 37 (38, 39)cm from cast-on edge, ending with a WS row.

Now set colours for neck stripes as folls:

Next row (RS): Patt 59 (64, 69)A, k2B, patt 59 (64, 69)A.

Next row (WS): Patt 59 (64, 69)A, p2B, patt 59(64,69)A.

Next row: Patt 58 (63, 68)A, k4B, patt 58 (63, 69)A.

Next row: Patt 58 (63, 68)A, p4B, patt 58 (63, 68)A.

Continue in this way, working 1 st less each side in A and 2 sts more in B on every alt row until the row with p10B in centre has been worked.

Next row: Patt 54 (59, 64)A, k5B, k2C, k5B, patt 54 (59, 64)A.

Next row: Patt 54 (59, 64)A, p5B, p2C, p5B, patt 54 (59, 64)A.

Continue in this way, working 1 st less each side in A and 2 sts more in C on every alternate row until the row with p10C in centre has been worked.

Divide for neck

Next row (RS): Patt 49 (54, 59)A, k5B, k4C, using C k2tog, turn and leave remaining sts on a stitch holder.

Next row (WS): P5C, p5B, patt 49 (54, 59)A.

Next row: Patt 48 (53, 58)A, k5B, k4C, using C work 2 tog.

Next row: P5C, p5B, patt 48 (53, 58)A.

Continue in this way, working 1 st less in A and working 2 tog in C on every alt row until 43 (48, 53) sts remain.

Work straight in colours and patt as set until front measures same as back to shoulder, ending at armhole edge.

Shape shoulder

Cast off 21 (24, 27) sts at beg of next row.
Work 1 row, then cast off.
Return to remaining sts.
With RS facing, join C, k2 tog, k4C, k5B, patt 49 (54, 59)A.

Next row: Patt 49 (54, 59)A, p5B, p5C.

Complete to match first side of neck, reversing all shaping.

SLEEVES

Using 3.25mm needles and A, cast on 56 (60, 60) sts.

Work 12cm in [k2, p2] rib and inc 1 st at each end of last row. 58 (62, 62) sts

Change to 4mm needles.

Using B and beg with RS knit row, work 6 rows in st st, increasing 1 st at each end of first and 3rd row. 62 (66, 66) sts.

Using C, work 6 rows in st st, increasing 1 st at each end of first and 3rd row. 66 (70, 70) sts

Continue in A only and increasing 1 st at each end, work 1 row st st. 68 (72, 72) sts

Foundation row (WS): P8 (10, 10) sts, [k2, p8] 5 times, k2, p8 (10, 10).

Work patt as folls:

Row 1 (RS): K8 (10, 10) sts, [p2, C8F, p2, k8] twice, p2, C8F, p2, k8 (10, 10).

Row 2 (WS): P8 (10, 10) sts, [k2, p8] 5 times, k2, p8 (10, 10).

Row 3: Kfb, k7 (9, 9), p2, [k8, p2] 5 times, k7 (9, 9), kfb. 2 sts inc

Row 4: P9 (11, 11) sts, [k2, p8] 5 times, k2, p9 (11, 11).

Row 5: K9 (11, 11), p2, [k8, p2] 5 times, k9 (11, 11).

Row 6: As row 4.

Row 7: Kfb, k8 (10, 10), p2, [k8, p2] 5 times, k8 (10, 10), kfb. 2 sts inc

Row 8: P10 (12, 12) sts, [k2, p8] 5 times, k2, p10 (12, 12).

Row 9: K10 (12, 12), p2, [k8, p2] 5 times, k10 (12, 12).

Row 10: As row 8.

Continue in patt increasing and working into st st 1 st at each end of next and every foll 4th row to 108 (112, 114) sts.

Work straight until sleeve measures 55 (56, 57)cm from cast-on edge, ending with a WS row.

Cast off.

NECKBAND

Join right shoulder seam, taking care to match stripes.

With RS facing, using 3.25mm needles and A, pick up and k52 sts down left side of front neck, pick up loop between sts at centre of 'V' and k into back of it, then mark this st. with a locking stitch marker to denote centre st, pick up and k52 sts up right side of front neck, then k across 34 sts from back neck holder. 139 sts

Rib row 1 (WS): [P2, k2] to within 2 sts of centre st, p2 tog, p centre st, p2 tog, [k2, p2] to end.

Rib row 2 (RS): Rib to within 2 sts of centre st, p2 tog, k centre st, p2 tog, rib to end.

Rep these 2 rows twice more.

Cast off in rib, decreasing each side of centre st. as before.

TO MAKE UP

Join left shoulder and neckband seam, matching stripes on shoulder.

Place markers approximately 27 (28, 29)cm below shoulder seams on back and front to denote beg of armholes.

Sew in sleeves between markers, then, matching stripes, join side and sleeve seams.

Cary Grant

A	56	(61,	66)	cm		F	54	(56,	57)	cm
	22	(24,	26)	in			21¼	(22,	22½)	in
B	60	(61,	62)	cm		G	29	(31,	31)	cm
	23½	(24,	24½)	in			11½	(12¼,	12¼)	in
C	9			cm		H	43	(44,	45)	cm
	3½			in			17	(17½,	17¾)	in
D	17			cm		I	12			cm
	6¾			in			4¾			in
E	25			cm						
	9¾			in						

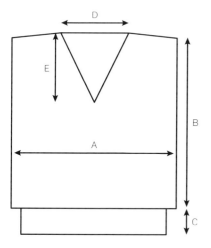

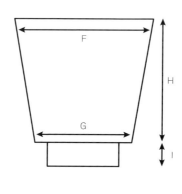

Cary Grant
1904 – 1986

Mae West always claimed that she discovered Cary Grant, and although he had made earlier films, it did his career no harm to appear in movies with the blatantly sexy Mae. One of the most popular actors ever to grace the screen, to his vast array of fans he was the embodiment of health, casual elegance and boyish charm. Such films as *Bringing Up Baby* (1938) with Katharine Hepburn and *The Awful Truth* (1937) with Irene Dunne saw Grant excel as an actor of considerable skill in a combination of sophisticated slapstick and pure romance.

Later, working with film director Alfred Hitchcock, he added another dimension to his expertise by portraying a callous schemer in *Suspicion* (1941) with co-star Joan Fontaine. His long association with Hitchcock produced some of his most memorable movies, notably *To Catch a Thief* (1955) with Grace Kelly and *North by Northwest* (1959) co-starring Eva Marie Saint. Cary Grant was one of Hitchcock's favourite leading men since he was a perfect foil for the typical cool blondes preferred by this masterly director.

In his private life, Grant had an air of restlessness, with four marriages ending quickly in divorce, though his fifth and last was long and happy. Later he was content to abandon the silver screen for the world of big business, and became a very rich man – quite an achievement for the English lad called Archibald Leach who ran away from home at the age of 13 to seek fame and fortune. Nevertheless, he will always be remembered for *le style 'sporty'* and the clean-cut suits that labelled him as one of the most dapper actors ever to grace the screen.

Jane Greer

Greer's sophisticated cotton cardigan shown on page 50 with short sleeves and a V-neck is worked in stocking stitch with a ribbed yoke. The collar and button borders are worked in horizontal rib using a circular needle. Shoulder pads give the cardigan an elegant line.

MEASUREMENTS

To fit bust: 81 (86, 91, 97, 102)cm
32 (34, 36, 38, 40)in

Actual measurements:
86 (91, 96, 102, 106)cm

Length to shoulders:
56 (57, 58, 59, 60)cm

Sleeve seam:
16cm

See schematic for full measurements.

MATERIALS

Sirdar Rafaella (50g)
   6 (6, 7, 7, 8) balls
A pair each of 2.75mm (UK 12)
   and 3.75mm (UK 9) knitting
   needles
A set of 2.75mm (UK 12) circular
   needles, 100cm (32in) long
Stitch holders
5 buttons
Shoulder pads

TENSION

24 sts and 32 rows to 10cm over st st using 3.75mm needles.

BACK

Using 2.75mm needles, cast on 99 (105, 111, 117, 123) sts.
Rib row 1 (RS): K1, *p1, k1; rep from * to end.
Rib row 2 (WS): P1, *k1, p1; rep from * to end. Rep these 2 rows for 5cm, ending with rib row 1.
Inc row (WS): Rib 20 (22, 22, 22, 26), *M1, rib 20 (20, 22, 24, 24); rep from * to last 19 (23, 23, 23, 25) sts, M1, rib to end. 103 (109, 115, 121, 127) sts
Change to 3.75mm needles.
Beg with a RS knit row, work in st st until back measures 36cm from cast-on edge, ending with a RS row.
Next row (WS): P1, *k1, p1; rep from * to end.
Shape armholes
Keeping rib patt correct, cast off 4 sts at beg of next 2 rows. 95 (101, 107, 113, 119) sts
Dec 1 st at each end of next and every foll alt row until 85 (89, 93, 97, 101) sts remain. Work straight until armholes measure 20 (21, 22, 23, 24)cm from beg of shaping, ending with a WS row.
Shape shoulders
Cast off 8 (8, 9, 9, 10) sts at beg of next 4 rows, then 8 (9, 9, 10, 10) sts at beg of next 2 rows. Break yarn and leave remaining 37 (39, 39, 41, 41) sts on a stitch holder.

LEFT FRONT

Using 2.75mm needles, cast on 44 (48, 50, 54, 56) sts.
Work [k1, p1] rib for 5cm, ending with a RS row.

Inc row (WS): Rib 12 (12, 14, 14, 14), *M1, rib 11 (24, 12, 26, 14); rep from * to last 10 (12, 12, 14, 14) sts, M1, rib to end. 47 (50, 53, 56, 59) sts
Change to 3.75mm needles.
Beg with a RS knit row, work in st st until front measures 6 rows less than back to beg of armhole shaping.
Shape front edge
Next row: K to last 3 sts, k2tog, k1. 46 (49, 52, 55, 58) sts
Work 3 rows straight.
Next row: K to last 3 sts, k2tog, k1. 45 (48, 51, 54, 57) sts
Next row: P1 (0, 1, 0, 1), *k1, p1; rep from * to end.
Continue in rib as now set and shape armhole and front edge as follows:
Row 1: Cast off 4 sts, rib to end.
Row 2: Rib to end.
Row 3: Work 2 sts tog, rib to last 2 sts, work 2 sts tog.
Row 4: Rib to end.
Row 5: Work 2 tog, rib to end.
Row 6: Rib to end.
Rep rows 3-6 until 33 (35, 36, 38, 39) sts remain, ending with row 4 (6, 4, 6, 4).
Keeping armhole edge straight, continue to dec at front edge until 24 (25, 27, 28, 30) sts remain.
Work straight until armhole measures same as back to shoulder, ending at armhole edge.
Shape shoulder
Cast off 8 (8, 9, 9, 10) sts at beg of next and foll alt row.
Work 1 row. Cast off.

RIGHT FRONT

Work as left front, reversing all shaping.

SLEEVES

Using 2.75mm needles cast on 71 (71, 73, 73, 75) sts.

Work the 2 rib rows for 4cm, ending with rib row 2.

Change to 3.75mm needles.

Continue in rib, inc and working into rib 1 st at each end of next and every foll 3rd row to 83 (87, 91, 95, 99) sts.

Work straight until sleeve measures 16cm from cast-on edge, ending with a WS row.

Shape top

Cast off 4 sts in rib at beg of next 2 rows. 75 (79, 83, 87, 91) sts

Dec 1 st at each end of next and every foll 4th row until 57 (61, 65, 69, 73) sts remain, then every foll alt row until 55 sts remain, ending with a WS row.

Cast off 2 sts in rib at beg of next 4 rows, 4 sts at beg of next 4 rows, then 6 sts at beg of next 2 rows.

Cast off remaining 19 sts.

FRONT BORDER AND COLLAR

Join shoulder seams.

With RS facing and using the 2.75mm circular needle, pick up and k95 sts evenly up right hand front to beg of front edge shaping and 63 (65, 69, 71, 75) sts up neck edge to shoulder, k across back neck sts from holder as follows: rib 5 (6, 6, 6, 6), [M1, rib 4] 7 times, M1, rib 4 (5, 5, 7, 7), pick up and k63 (65, 69, 71, 75) sts evenly down left front neck to beg of shaping and 95 sts down left front to lower edge. 361 (367, 375, 381, 389) sts

Beg with rib row 2, work 4 rows in rib.

Shape collar

Next row (WS): Rib 260 (266, 274, 280, 288), turn.

Next row (RS): Sl 1, rib 158 (164, 172, 178, 186), turn.

Next row: Sl 1, rib 152 (158, 166, 172, 180), turn.

Continue in this way, working 6 sts less on every row, until 24 rows have been worked from beg of shaping.

Next row: Sl 1, rib to end.

Next row: Rib to end.

Buttonhole row 1: Rib to last 85 sts, cast off 2 sts, *rib 18, cast off 2 sts; rep from * a further 3 times, rib to end.

Buttonhole row 2: Rib to end, casting on 2 sts over those cast off in previous row.

Work 6 rows in rib.

Cast off loosely in rib.

TO MAKE UP

Do not press. Sew in sleeves, Join side and sleeve seams. Sew on buttons.

Sew in shoulder pads.

A	43	(45.5,	48,	51,	53)	cm
	17	(18,	19,	20,	21)	in
B	20	(21,	22,	23,	24)	cm
	7¾	(8¼,	8¾,	9,	9½)	in
C	31	cm				
	12¼	in				
D	5	cm				
	2	in				
E	15	(16,	16,	17,	17)	cm
	6	(6¼,	6¼,	6¾,	6¾)	in
F	35	(37,	38,	40,	42)	cm
	13¾	(14½,	15,	15¾,	16¼)	in

G	19.5	(21,	22,	23,	24)	cm
	7¾	(8¼,	8¾,	9,	9½)	in
H	34	cm				
	13½	in				
I	34	(36,	37,	39,	41)	cm
	13½	(14,	14½,	15½,	16)	in
J	16	cm				
	6¼	in				
K	29	(29,	30,	30,	31)	cm
	11½	(11½,	12,	12,	12¼)	in

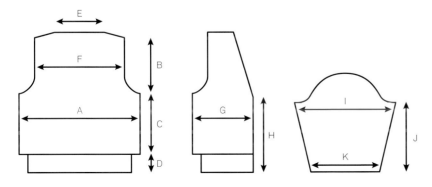

Jane Greer
1924 – 2001

Hollywood needed villainesses as well as heroines and Bettejane Greer, as Jane Greer was born, seemed to fit the bill to perfection. Pushed by an ambitious, stage-struck mother, Bettejane was modelling professionally at 12, and later worked as a vocalist, singing Latin-American numbers in a Washington night club.

During one of her modelling assignments she caught the attention of the elusive Howard Hughes, who put her under contract, but after a year no suitable roles had been found for her. In 1943, she married crooner Rudy Vallee who secured her a contract with RKO studios. The marriage was short-lived but her career took an upswing. She soon graduated from B movies to more prestigious roles, often still cast as the villainess but excelling as the classic *femme fatale*. One of the most notable of her films was *Out of the Past* (1947) with Robert Mitchum. In the 1952 version of *The Prisoner of Zenda* with Stewart Granger and Deborah Kerr, she played Michael, Duke of Strelsau's (Robert Douglas) love interest, coming to a sticky end. She looked beautiful in the film, her dark and romantic appearance providing a perfect foil for Miss Kerr's English rose.

From leopard skin print dresses to 'sassy' period costumes, she always had style and flair. Her modelling experience gave her poise and a natural ease, enabling her to show off a garment to its best advantage. However, she chose to semi-retire from the screen in 1953 to raise a family, taking on smaller film roles in the 60s and 70s and appearing in television dramas, including *Twin Peaks*, in the 80s and 90s.

Jean Harlow

This button-fronted sweater with collar has set-in sleeves in a choice of lengths. Both versions, long- or short-sleeved, have double-rib cuffs to match the welt. The single-rib collar is knitted separately and sewn on afterwards.

MEASUREMENTS

To fit bust:
81 (86, 91, 97)cm
32 (34, 36, 38)in

Actual measurements:
96 (102, 108, 114)cm

Length to shoulders:
57 (58, 59, 60)cm

Sleeve seam – short:
10cm

Sleeve seam – long:
48 (49, 50, 51)cm

See schematic for full measurements.

MATERIALS

Bergère de France Lima (50g balls)

Short sleeved version:
9 (9, 10, 10) balls

Long sleeved version:
10 (12, 12, 13) balls

A pair each of 2.75mm (UK 12), 3mm (UK 11) and 3.75mm (UK 9) knitting needles
Stitch holders
5 buttons

TENSION

22 sts and 31 rows to 10cm over st st using 3.75mm needles.

BACK

Using 2.75mm needles, cast on 100 (106, 110, 116) sts.
Work 6cm in [k2, p2] rib, ending with a RS row.
Inc row (WS): Rib 5 (8, 3, 6), *kfb, rib 14 (14, 12, 12); rep from * to last 5 (8, 3, 6) sts, kfb, rib to end. 107 (113, 119, 125) sts
Change to 3.75mm needles.
Beg with a RS knit row, work in st st until back measures 33cm from cast-on edge, ending with a WS row.

Shape armholes

Cast off 3 (3, 3, 4) sts at beg of next 2 rows, 2 (2, 3, 3) sts at beg of next 2 rows, then 2 sts at beg of foll 2 (6, 6, 6) rows. 93 (91, 95, 99) sts
Dec 1 st at beg of next 8 (4, 4, 6) rows. 85 (87, 91, 93) sts
Work straight until back measures 54 (55, 56, 57)cm from cast-on edge, ending with a WS row.

Shape shoulders and neck

Cast off 5 (6, 6, 6) sts at beg of next 2 rows and 6 sts at beg of foll 2 rows. 63 (63, 67, 69) sts
Next row (RS): Cast off 6 (6, 6, 7) sts, k16 (16, 18, 18) sts (including st left on needle after cast-off), cast off next 19 sts, k to end.
Continue on first set of 22 (22, 24, 25) sts as folls:
Next row (WS): Cast off 6 (6, 6, 7) sts, p to end.

Next row (RS): Cast off 10 (10, 11, 11) sts, k to end.
Cast off remaining 6 (6, 7, 7) sts.
With WS facing, rejoin yarn to remaining sts and p to end.
Complete to match first side of neck, reversing all shaping.

FRONT

Work as given for Back until front measures 29 (30, 31, 32)cm, ending with a WS row.
Divide for front opening
Next row (RS): K50 (53, 56, 59), cast off next st, k to end.
Continue on last set of sts for right front as follows:

1st and 2nd sizes only
Next row (WS): P to end.
Next row (RS): Cast off 2 sts, k to end.
P 1 row, then cast off 1 st at neck edge on next row, 2 sts on foll alt row and 1 st on foll alt row.
Work 2 (4) rows straight, so ending at armhole edge.
Shape armhole
Cast off 3 sts at beg of next row and 2 sts at beg of foll 2 (4) alt rows.
Dec 1 st at armhole edge on foll 4 (2) alt rows: 39 (40) sts

3rd size only
Next row (WS): P to end.
Next row (RS): Cast off 2 sts, k to end.
P 1 row, then cast off 1 st at neck edge on next row and 2 sts on foll alt row.

Adele Jergens

A sexy, bare-midriff top knitted in fluffy angora that will show off your tan even on cooler days. The short top with slightly gathered, set-in sleeves and round neck is quick to knit in basic stocking stitch, but the effect is glamorous.

MEASUREMENTS

To fit bust:
81 (86, 91, 97)cm
32 (34, 36, 38)in

Actual measurements:
84 (88, 94, 98)cm

Length to shoulders:
34 (34, 37, 37)cm

Sleeve seam:
8cm

See schematic for full measurements.

MATERIALS

Orkney Angora St Magnus
   (50g balls) 3 (3, 3, 4) balls
A pair each of 4mm (UK 8) and
   4.5mm (UK 7) knitting needles
Stitch holders

TENSION

20 sts and 30 rows to 10cm over st st using 4.5mm needles.

BACK

**Using 4mm needles, cast on 69 (73, 79, 83) sts.
Rib row 1 (RS): K1, *p1, k1; rep from * to end.
Rib row 2 (WS): P1, *k1, p1; rep from * to end.
Rep these 2 rows for 3cm, ending with rib row 1.
Inc row (WS): Rib 6 (8, 4, 6), *M1, rib 4 (4, 5, 5); rep from * to last 7 (9, 5, 7) sts, M1, rib to end. 84 (88, 94, 98) sts
Change to 4.5mm needles.
Starting with a RS knit row, work in st st until back measures 15 (15, 17, 17)cm from cast-on edge, ending with a WS row.

Shape armholes

Cast off 6 sts at beg of next 2 rows. 72 (76, 82, 86) sts
Dec 1 st each end of every row until 60 (60, 64, 64) sts remain.**
Work straight until armholes measure 19 (19, 20, 20)cm from armhole cast-off, ending with a WS row.

Shape shoulders

Cast off 9 (9, 10, 10) sts at beg of next 4 rows.
Break yarn and leave remaining 24 sts on a stitch holder.

FRONT

Work as given for Back from ** to **.

Work straight until armholes measure 13 (13, 14, 14)cm from armhole cast-off, ending with a WS row.

Shape neck

Next row (RS): K24 (24, 26, 26), turn and leave remaining sts on a stitch holder.
Work 1 row.
Dec 1 st at neck edge on next and every foll alt row until 18 (18, 20, 20) sts remain.
Work straight until front measures same as back to shoulders, ending at armhole edge.

Shape shoulder

Cast off 9 (9, 10, 10) sts at beg of next row.
Work 1 row. Cast off remaining 9 (9, 10, 10) sts.
Return to held sts.
With RS facing, leaving first 12 sts on holder, rejoin yarn and work second side of neck to match first, reversing all shaping.

SLEEVES

Using 4mm needles cast on 49 (49, 53, 53) sts.
Work the 2 rib rows for 3cm, ending with rib row 1.
Inc row (WS): Rib 2 (2, 4, 4), *M1, rib 3; rep from * to last 2 (2, 4, 4) sts, M1, rib to end. 65 (65, 69, 69) sts
Change to 4.5mm needles.
Starting with a RS knit row, work in st st until work measures 8cm from cast-on edge, ending with a WS row.

yarn and leave remaining sts on a stitch holder.

BACK

Omitting front opening work as given for Front until back measures the same as front to armholes, ending with a WS row.

Shape armholes

Cast off 2 (2, 3) sts at beg of next 2 rows.
Dec 1 st at each end of next and every foll 6th row until 47 (49, 49) sts remain, then each end of every row until 33 sts remain, ending with a WS row.
Cast off 8 sts, patt to last 8 sts, cast off these 8 sts.
Break yarn and leave remaining 17 sts on a stitch holder.

SLEEVES

Using 6mm needles and yarn held double, cast on 41 sts. Change to 8mm needles.
Row 1: With yf, sl1, *yb, k1, yf, sl1; rep from * to end.
Row 2: K1, *yf, sl1, yb, k1; rep from * to end.
Rep these 2 rows once more.
Continue to work in rib patt as given for front until sleeve measures 10cm from cast-on edge, ending with a RS row.
Change to 6mm needles.
Patt 3 rows.
Next row: P1, *k1B, p1; rep from * to end.
Next row: K to end.
Rep the last 2 rows twice more.
Change to 8mm needles and continue in patt, increasing and working into rib patt 1 st each end of next and every foll 4th row to 55 (61, 67) sts.
Work straight until sleeve measures 41cm from cast-on edge, ending with a WS row.

Shape top

Cast off 2 sts at beg of next 2 rows.
Dec 1 st each end of next and every foll alt row until 11 sts remain, ending with a RS row.
Mark end of last row with a locking stitch marker for left sleeve and at beg of last row

for right sleeve.
Keeping marked edge straight, continue decreasing at other edge until 7 sts remain.
Work straight until straight edge is long enough, when slightly stretched, to fit along shoulder section of front.
Break yarn and leave remaining sts on a holder.

BUTTONHOLE BAND

With RS facing, using 6mm needles, pick up and k47 sts up right side of front opening.
Beg with rib row 1, work 5 rows rib as given for front.
Buttonhole row 1: Rib 4, *cast off next st, rib 9; rep from * a further 3 times, cast off next st, rib to end.
Buttonhole row 2: Rib to end, casting on 1 st over those cast off in previous row.
Work 4 more rows in rib.
Cast off in rib.

BUTTON BAND

With RS facing, pick up and k47 sts down left side of neck opening.
Work 9 rows in rib.
Cast off in rib.

COLLAR

With RS facing, using 6mm needles, pick up and k4 sts across top of buttonhole band, patt 6 sts up right side of neck, 7 sts across right sleeve top, 17 sts along back neck, 7 sts along left sleeve top, 6 sts down left side of neck, then pick up and k4 sts along button band. 51 sts
K 1 row.

Shape collar

Next 2 rows: Patt to last 20 sts, turn and k to last 20 sts, turn.
Next 2 rows: Patt to last 18 sts, turn and k to last 18 sts, turn.
Next 2 rows: Patt to last 16 sts, turn and k to last 16 sts, turn.
Continue in this way, working 2 more sts before turning on every 2 rows until all the sts of collar have been worked.

Continue in patt over all sts until front edge of collar measures 46cm, ending at buttonhole band edge.
Next 2 rows: K to last st, turn and patt to last st, turn.
Next 2 rows: K to last 3 sts, turn and patt, to last 3 sts, turn.
Next 2 rows: K to last 5 sts, turn and patt to last 5 sts, turn.
Continue in this way, working 2 sts less each end until 2 rows have been worked as follows: k to last 19 sts, turn and patt to last 19 sts, turn.
Next row: K to end, so ending at button band edge.
Work 1 more row over all sts.
Cast off loosely in patt.

TO MAKE UP

Join raglan seams, fitting the side edges of sleeve top to cast-off sts along shoulder sections of back and front.
Turn collar in half to wrong side and slipstitch into position.
Join side and sleeve seams, reversing cuff seams for last 10cm.
Stitch lower edges of front bands to cast-off sts at centre front.
Work a row of double crochet along front edges of collar, working through both thicknesses.
Make a button loop on right front edge of collar approximately 7cm up from buttonhole band.
Sew on buttons to correspond with buttonholes, and one button onto underside of collar, approximately 7cm up from button band and 3cm in from the edge, to correspond with button loop.

holder, then pick up and k16 sts up left side of back neck. 184 (192, 200, 208) sts

Work 7 rows in [k2, p2] rib.

Cast off in rib.

TO MAKE UP

Join left back raglan and neckband seam.

Join side and sleeve seams.

BEADING

Most types of beads can be used in beaded embroidery, as long as the hole is large enough to accommodate the thread. Avoid beads that are very large or heavy because they may pull the knitting out of shape, or even pull a hole. You may need lightweight interfacing on the back to support the beads. Check that the beads you want to use do not have sharp edges anywhere that may cut or catch on the yarn. Plastic beads may melt if the item needs to be pressed and some wooden beads may not be colourfast. Be aware of the laundering requirements for yarn, thread and beads – washing may not be an option for very complex beading or yarns that shrink, but some beads may not stand up to dry cleaning chemicals very well.

Once you have chosen your beads, work out the spacing you need between the bead motifs so that they sit evenly. In this garment a line of stylized flowers has been created with single green bugle beads forming stems, while clusters of smaller beads (consisting of two rows of two sandwiching a row of three beads) are couched in place to form flower heads. When sewing on single beads or couching, most of the thread will be covered by the bead itself, so you can use ordinary hand sewing thread to match your yarn. See page 92 for instructions on bead embroidery.

A	46	(48,	51,	53)	cm
	18	*(19,*	*20,*	*21)*	*in*
B	24	(24,	26,	26)	cm
	9½	*(9½,*	*10¼,*	*10¼)*	*in*
C	5	cm			
	2	*in*			
D	25	(27,	28,	30)	cm
	9¾	*(10¾,*	*11,*	*12)*	*in*
E	2.5	cm			
	1	*in*			
F	14	(14.5,	15,	15.5)	cm
	5½	*(5¾,*	*6,*	*6¼)*	*in*
G	32.5	(33,	34,	35)	cm
	12¾	*(13,*	*13½,*	*13¾)*	*in*
H	15.5	(16,	17,	17.5)	cm
	6¼	*(6½,*	*6¾,*	*7)*	*in*
I	4.5	cm			
	1¾	*in*			
J	2.5	cm			
	1	*in*			
K	13	cm			
	5¼	*in*			
L	29	(30,	31,	32)	cm
	11½	*(12,*	*12¼,*	*12¾)*	*in*

Dorothy Lamour

1914 – 1996

In a studio photograph taken in 1936 by Ernest A. Bachrach, Dorothy Lamour's features, although she was brunette, are not dissimilar to those of pop star Madonna at the same age. Indeed, Lamour started her career as a singer in Chicago. Her slightly exotic looks led to her first movie *The Jungle Princess* (1936), and she was to spend most of her film career in exotic settings draped in a sarong. Although she begged the studio to consider her for more substantial roles, Miss Lamour and the sarong were big box office. When the US marines were engaged in warfare in the South Pacific, Dorothy epitomised their ideal South Sea Island Beauty.

Her most memorable films were the *Road* series: *Road to Singapore* (1940), *Road to Zanzibar* (1941), *Road to Morocco* (1942), *Road to Utopia* (1945), *Road to Rio* (1947) and *Road to Bali* (1952). Teamed with the dynamic duo Bing Crosby and Bob Hope, these successful movies made her a household name, which was good news for the ex-Miss New Orleans (1931), where she was born. The chemistry between Lamour and Hope brought out a special ingredient in her that transcended the ordinary.

She had a voluptuous figure, carried herself well, always looking good, and had the enviable ability to make a potato sack look like a couture garment. She was a great success in one of the touring versions of *Hello, Dolly!* in the 1960s and appeared frequently on TV, but she refused to do another movie until she was offered more interesting material – without her trademark sarong.

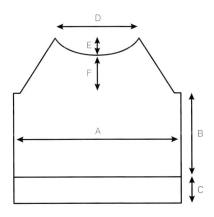

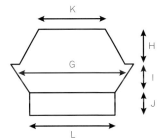

Virginia Mayo

This picture sweater in stocking stitch is not strictly for the birds! The motif is echoed on the back, with the set-in sleeves left plain. The welts and decorative armhole borders are in double rib, with the neckband slipstitched inside to give a neat finish.

MEASUREMENTS

To fit bust:
81 (86, 91, 97)cm
32 (34, 36, 38)in

Actual measurements:
91 (96, 101, 106)cm

Length to shoulders:
54 (54.5, 55, 55.5)cm

Sleeve seam:
42 (42, 43, 43)cm

See schematic for full measurements.

MATERIALS

Rowan Pure Wool DK (50g balls)
  8 (9, 9, 10) balls in main colour A
  1 ball in each contrast colour
    B, C and D
A pair each of 3.25mm (UK 10)
    and 4mm (UK 8) knitting needles
Stitch holders x 2

TENSION

22 sts and 30 rows to 10cm over st st using 4mm needles.

FRONT

**With 3.25mm needles and A, cast on 78 (86, 90, 98) sts.
Rib row 1: K2, *p2, k2; rep from * to end.
Rib row 2: P2, *k2, p2; rep from * to end.
Rep these 2 rows for 8cm, ending with rib row 1.
Inc row (WS): Rib 6 (7, 7, 8), *M1, rib 6 (8, 7, 9); rep from * to last 6 (7, 6, 9) sts, M1, rib 6 (7, 6, 9). 90 (96, 102, 108) sts**
Change to 4mm needles.
Note: When working the contrast colour patt, use separate small balls of yarn for each area of contrast colour and twist yarns together on WS of work when changing colours to avoid making a hole.
Starting with a RS knit row and working in st st throughout, reading odd numbered (knit) rows from right to left and even numbered (purl) rows from left to right, work in patt from chart increasing 1 st at each end of every 10th row to 100 (106, 112, 118) sts.
Continue in patt from chart until row 80 has been completed.

Shape armholes

Continuing to work patt as set, cast off 6 (7,8,9) sts at beg of next 2 rows.
Keeping patt correct, dec 1 st at each end of every foll row until 76 (80, 84, 88) sts remain, then every foll alt row until 72 (76, 80, 84) sts remain.
Work straight until row 113 of chart has been completed.

Working in A only, continue in st st for a further 7 (7, 11, 11) rows.

Shape neck

Next row (RS): K27 (29,31,33) sts, turn and leave remaining sts on a stitch holder.
Work on first set of sts as follows:
Dec 1 st at neck edge on next 4 rows, then on every foll alt row until 19 (20, 21, 22) sts remain.
Work 5 (5, 1, 1) rows straight, ending at armhole edge.

Shape shoulders

Cast off 10 sts at beg of next row.
Work 1 row. Cast off.
With RS facing, leaving first 18 sts on a holder, rejoin yarn and k to end.
Complete to match first side of neck, reversing all shaping.

BACK

Work as given for Front from ** to **.
Change to 4mm needles.
Working in A only, inc 1 st at each end of every 10th row to 100 (106, 112, 118) sts.
Starting with a RS knit row, work straight in st st for 80 rows.

Shape armholes

Cast off 6 (7, 8, 9) sts at beg of next 2 rows.
Dec 1 st each end of every row until 76 (80, 84, 88) sts remain, then on every foll alt row until 72 (76, 80, 84) sts remain, ending with a WS row.
Work 10 rows straight.
Beg with RS row 93 of chart, work bird

FRONT AND BACK
A (Main colour)
B (Contrast colour)
C (Contrast colour)
D (Contrast colour)

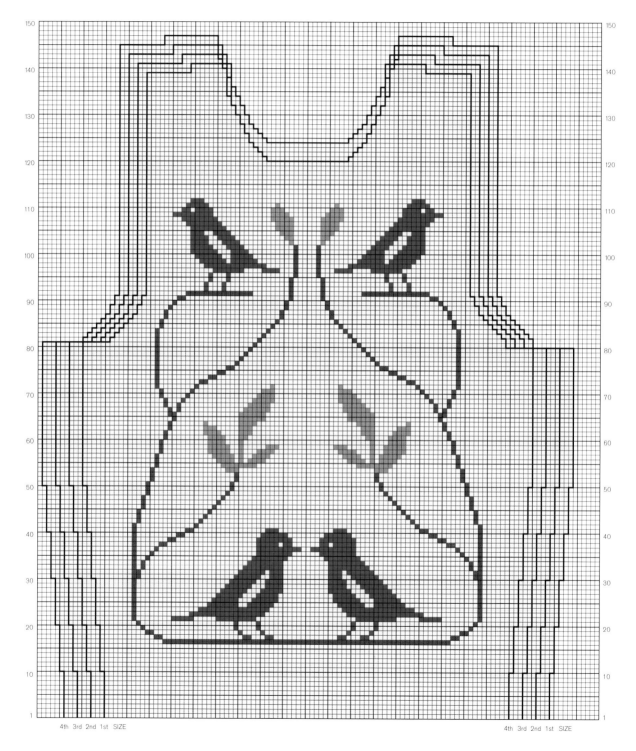

4th 3rd 2nd 1st SIZE

4th 3rd 2nd 1st SIZE

motifs **only** in contrast colour D, omitting leaves and stems.
Continue as set to end of row 113 has been completed.
Work straight until back measures same as front to shoulders, ending with a WS row.

Shape shoulders

Cast off 10 sts at beg of next 2 rows and 9 (10, 11, 12) sts at beg of foll 2 rows.
Break yarn and leave remaining 34 (36, 38, 40) sts on a holder.

SLEEVES

Using 3.25mm needles and A, cast on 44 (48, 52, 56) sts.
Work in [k2, p2] rib for 8cm, ending with a RS row.

Inc row (WS): Rib 2 (6, 1, 4), *M1, rib 4 (4, 5, 5); rep from * to last 2 (2, 1, 2) sts, rib 2 (2, 1, 2). 54 (58, 62, 66) sts
Change to 4mm needles.
Starting with a RS knit row, work in st st increasing 1 st at each end of 5th and every foll 6th row to 84 (88, 92, 96) sts.
Work straight until sleeve measures 42 (42, 43, 43)cm, ending with a WS row.

Shape top

Cast off 6 (7, 8, 9) sts at beg of next 2 rows.
Dec 1 st at each end of next 6 rows, then 1 st at each end of every foll alt row until 38 sts remain.
Dec 1 st at each end of every row until 22 sts remain.
Cast off 4 sts at beg of next 2 rows, then cast off remaining 14 sts.

NECKBAND

Join right shoulder seam.
With RS facing, using 3.25mm needles and A, pick up and k18 (19, 20, 21) sts down left front neck, k across 18 sts from front neck holder, pick up and k18 (19, 20, 21) sts up right side of front neck, then k across 34 (36, 38, 40) sts from back neck holder. 88 (92, 96, 100) sts
Work 6cm in [k2, p2] rib.
Cast off in rib.

ARMHOLE BORDERS

Using 3.25mm needles and A, cast on 128(132,136,140) sts
Work 4 rows in [k2, p2] rib.
Cast off 8 sts at beg of next 6 rows.
Cast off in rib.

TO MAKE UP

Join left shoulder and neckband seam.
Fold neckband in half to wrong side and slipstitch into place.
Tack cast off edges of armhole borders round armhole, then sew in sleeves stitching through all three thicknesses.
Join side and sleeve seams.
Press lightly following instructions on ball band.

A	45.5	(48,	50.5,	53)	cm
	18	(19,	19¾,	21)	in
B	19.5	(20,	20.5,	21)	cm
	7½	(7¾,	8,	8¼)	in
C	26.5				cm
	10½				in
D	8				cm
	3¼				in
E	15	(16,	17,	18)	cm
	5¾	(6¼,	6¾,	7¼)	in
F	6				cm
	2¼				in
G	33	(34.5,	36,	38)	cm
	13	(13½,	14¼,	15)	in
H	41	(44,	46,	49)	cm
	16	(17½,	18,	19¼)	in
I	38	(40,	42,	44)	cm
	15	(15¾,	16½,	17½)	in
J	34	(34,	35,	35)	cm
	13½	(13½,	13¾,	13¾)	in
K	8				cm
	3¼				in
L	24	(26,	28,	30)	cm
	9½	(10¼,	11,	12)	in

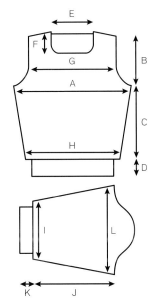

Marilyn Monroe

MEASUREMENTS

To fit bust:
81 (86, 91, 97)cm
32 (34, 36, 38)in

Actual measurements:
86 (90, 95, 99)cm

Length to shoulders:
51 (52, 53, 54)cm

*See schematic for full
measurements.*

MATERIALS

Debbie Bliss Baby Cashmerino
   (50g balls) 4 (5, 5, 6) balls
A pair each of 3.25mm (UK 10)
   and 4mm (UK 8) knitting needles
   Stitch holders x 2

TENSION

21 sts and 28 rows to 10cm over
st st using 4mm needles.

This quick-knit sleeveless top looks great layered or worn on its own. It's worked throughout in stocking stitch and the minimum shaping makes it a good choice for beginners. The round neckline has an unusual, deep single-rib neckband, pinned down asymmetrically with a brooch to great effect by Miss Monroe.

BACK

Using 3.25mm needles, cast on 76 (80, 86, 90)sts.
Work 7cm in [k1, p1] rib.
Change to 4mm needles.
Beg with a RS knit row, work in st st and dec 1 st at each end of first and every following 3rd row until 66 (70, 76, 80) sts remain ending with a RS row.
Work 3 rows straight.
Continue in st st and inc 1 st at each end of next and every following 4th row to 90 (94, 100, 104) sts.
Work straight until back measures 32 (32.5, 33, 33.5)cm from cast-on edge, ending with a WS row.

Shape armholes

Cast off 2 (3, 3, 4)sts at beg of next 2 rows. 86 (88, 94, 96) sts
Dec 1 st at each end of next 2 rows, then each end of every foll alt row until 76 (78, 82, 84) sts remain.
Work straight until back measures 51 (52, 53, 54)cm from cast-on edge, ending with a WS row.

Shape shoulders

Cast off 11 (11, 12, 12)sts at beg of next 2 rows, then 12 (12, 13, 13) sts at beg of foll 2 rows.
Break yarn and leave remaining 30 (32, 32, 34) sts on a holder.

FRONT

Work as given for back until front measures 42 (43, 43, 44)cm from cast-on edge, ending with a WS row.

Shape neck

Next row (RS): K34 (35, 37, 38), turn and leave remaining sts on a stitch holder.
Dec 1 st at neck edge on every row until 23 (23, 25, 25) sts remain.
Work straight until front measures same as back to shoulder, ending at armhole edge.

Shape shoulder

Cast off 11 (11, 12, 12) sts at beg of next row.
Work 1 row.
Cast off remaining 12 (12, 13, 13) sts.
With RS facing, and leaving first 8 sts on stitch holder, rejoin yarn to remaining sts and k to end.
Complete to match first side of neck, reversing all shaping.

Robert Taylor

Change to 4mm needles.
Work in patt as follows:
Row 1 (RS): K24 (26), *p1, k6, p1, k4;
rep from * to last 32 (34) sts, p1, k6, p1, k
to end.
Row 2 (WS): P24 (26), k1, p6, k1, *p4, k1,
p6, k1; rep from * to last 32 (34) sts, k1, p6,
k1, p to end.
Rows 3 and 4: As rows 1 and 2.
Row 5: K24 (26), *p1, C6F, p1, k4, rep
from * to last 32 (34) sts, p1, C6F, p1,
k to end.
Row 6: As row 2.
Rows 7 and 8: As rows 1 and 2.
These 8 rows form the patt.
Continue in patt until work measures
47 (48)cm from cast-on edge, ending with
a WS row.
Shape top
Cast off 4 sts at beg of next 2 rows and
2 sts at beg of next 4 rows. 88 (92) sts
Dec 1 st at beg of next 22 (26) rows.
66 (70) sts

Cast off 2 sts at beg of next 6 rows,
3 sts at beg of next 4 rows, 4 sts at beg
of next 2 rows, then 5 sts at beg of next
2 rows.
Cast off remaining 24 sts.

NECKBAND
Join right shoulder seam.
With RS facing, using 3.25mm needles,
pick up and k30 (31) sts down left side of
front neck, k across 16 (18) sts from front
neck holder, pick up and k30 (31) sts up
left side of front neck, then k across
46 (48) sts from back neck holder. 122
(128) sts
Work 2.5cm in [k1, p1] rib.
Cast off loosely in rib.

TO MAKE UP
Join left shoulder and neckband seam.
Sew in sleeves.
Join side and sleeve seams.
Press lightly foll instructions on ball band.

Robert Taylor
1911 – 1969

Robert Taylor, born with the
unlikely name of Spangler
Arlington Brugh in Filley, Nebraska,
was the son of a doctor. The
cello first attracted him, then the
stage, and eventually he was
signed by MGM to a seven-year
contract at the princely sum of
$35 a week. He was soon labelled
the 'Pretty Boy' of Hollywood, a
label he heartily disliked for he
was an actor who respected his
profession and always tried to
give his best. However, his good
looks did not hinder his career
and undoubtedly helped him
get a starring role opposite Greta
Garbo in *Camille* (1936) and
every other major female MGM
star for the next two decades.

Taylor was a consistent worker,
not wildly ambitious, and stayed
with MGM for 25 years. He made
many memorably romantic
movies such as *Waterloo Bridge*
(1940) with Vivien Leigh, *Quo
Vadis* (1951) with Deborah Kerr
and *Quentin Durward* (1955)
with Kay Kendall. His marriage to
one of his leading ladies, Barbara
Stanwyck, in 1939 lasted 13 years,
worth mentioning as its longevity
was unusual in Tinsel Town.

His striking and flawless
features were complemented
by a good physique and he was
equally at home in costume, or a
contemporary cable-knit pullover,
looking classically elegant in
both. His stunning good looks and
appealing modesty endeared
him to millions of female fans
throughout his career. Although
he would have denied it, he
became an institution, firmly
entrenched as one of the great
glamour stars of Hollywood.

A	50	(57)	cm
	20	(22½)	in
B	21.5	(23)	cm
	8½	(9¼)	in
C	26.5	(27.5)	cm
	10½	(11)	in
D	8		cm
	3¼		in
E	17	(18)	cm
	6¾	(7)	in
F	8		cm
	3¼		in
G	44	(50)	cm
	17½	(19½)	in
H	47	(53)	cm
	18½	(21)	in
I	28	(40)	cm
	11	(15¾)	in
J	39	(40)	cm
	15½	(15¾)	in
K	8		cm
	3¼		in

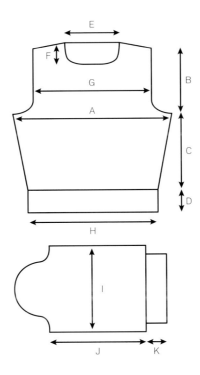

Lana Turner

MEASUREMENTS

To fit bust:
81 (86, 91, 97, 102)cm
32 (34, 36, 38, 40)in

Actual measurements:
85 (91, 96, 101, 107)cm

Length to shoulders:
50 (51, 52, 55, 57)cm

Sleeve seam:
11cm

*See schematic for full
measurements.*

MATERIALS

Bergère de France Coton à Tricoter
   (50g balls) 3 (4, 5, 5, 5) balls
A pair each of 2mm (UK 13) and
   3mm (UK 11) knitting needles
3mm (UK 11) crochet hook
Stitch holders

TENSION

30 sts and 38 rows to 10cm over
st st using 3mm needles.

This fitted short-sleeved summer top
made in cool crochet cotton has a
deep double-rib welt. The top is knitted
in basic stocking stitch with a front
neck opening and collar. The collar
is edged with double crochet to give
it shape, and the sleeves have pretty
crochet borders.

BACK

**Using 2mm needles, cast on 116 (120,
128, 136, 144) sts
Work 10cm in [k2, p2] rib.
Change to 3mm needles.
Beg with a RS knit row, work in st st and
inc 1 st at each end of 9th and every foll
8th row to 128 (136, 144, 152, 160) sts.
Work straight until back measures 33 (33,
33, 36, 37)cm, ending with a WS row.**

Shape armholes

Cast off 8 sts at beg of next 2 rows.
112 (120, 128, 136, 144) sts
Dec 1 st at each end of next and every foll
alt row until 98 (104, 110, 116, 122) sts
remain.
Work straight until armholes measure
17 (18, 19, 19, 20)cm from beg of shaping,
ending with a WS row.

Shape shoulders

Cast off 6 (6, 7, 7, 8) sts at beg of next
6 rows, then 5 (7, 6, 8, 7) sts at beg of foll
2 rows.
Break yarn and leave remaining 52 (54, 56,
58, 60) sts on a holder.

FRONT

Work as given for Back from ** to **.
Shape armholes and divide for front
opening:

Next row (RS): Cast off 8 sts, k60 (64,
68, 72, 76) sts, turn and leave remaining
60 (64, 68, 72, 76) sts on a stitch holder.
Continue on first set of sts as follows:
Next row (WS): Cast on 8 sts, p across
these 8 sts, then p7, k1, p to end.
Next row: K2tog, k to last 16 sts, p1,
k to end.
Continuing to work the 16th st from neck
edge in rev st st, dec 1 st at armhole edge
on every foll alt row until 61 (64, 67, 70, 73)
sts remain.
Keeping patt correct, work straight until
front measures 18 rows less than back
to beg of shoulder shaping, so ending at
armhole edge.

Shape neck

Next 2 rows: K to last 25 (26, 27, 28, 29)
sts, turn and p to end.
Next 2 rows: K to last 28 (29, 30, 31, 32)
sts, turn and p to end.
Next 2 rows: K to last 31 (32, 33, 34, 35)
sts, turn and p to end.
Next 2 rows: K to last 33 (34, 35, 36, 37)
sts, turn and p to end.
Next 2 rows: K to last 35 (36, 37, 38, 39)
sts, turn and p to end.
Next row: K23 (25, 27, 29, 31) sts, turn
and leave remaining sts on a holder.
Next row: P to end.

Lana Turner

Continue in st st on these sts until front measures same as back to beg of shoulder shaping, ending at armhole edge.

Shape shoulder

Cast off 6 (6, 7, 7, 8) sts at beg of next and foll 2 alt rows.

Work 1 row, then cast off remaining 5 (7, 6, 8, 7) sts.

Using 3mm needles cast on 2 sts for centre front border.

K 1 row and p 1 row.

Continuing in st st, inc 1 st at beg of next 6 rows. 8 sts

Work 2 rows in st st.

Return to remaining sts.

With RS facing, and using the needle holding the 8 border sts, k across sts from stitch holder for right side of neck. 68 (72, 76, 80, 84) sts

Shape armhole

Next row: Cast off 8 sts, p to last 8 sts, k1, p7, turn and cast on 8 sts for front border facing. 68 (72, 76, 80, 84) sts

Continuing to work the 16th st from neck edge in rev st st, dec 1 st at armhole edge on next and every foll alt row until 61 (64, 67, 70, 73) sts remain.

Keeping patt correct, work straight until front measures 18 rows less than back to beg of shoulder shaping, ending at armhole edge.

Shape neck

Next 2 rows: P to last 25 (26, 27, 28, 29) sts, turn and k to end.

Next 2 rows: P to last 28 (29, 30, 31, 32) sts, turn and k to end.

Next 2 rows: P to last 31 (32, 33, 34, 35) sts, turn and k to end.

Next 2 rows: P to last 33 (34, 35, 36, 37) sts, turn and k to end.

Next 2 rows: P to last 35 (36, 37, 38, 39) sts, turn and k to end.

Next row: P23 (25, 27, 29, 31) sts, turn and leave remaining sts on a holder.

Next row: K to end.

Continue in st st on these sts until front measures same as back to beg of shoulder shaping, ending at armhole edge.

Shape shoulder

Cast off 6 (6, 7, 7, 8) sts at beg of next and foll 2 alt rows.

Work 1 row, then cast off remaining 5 (7, 6, 8, 7) sts.

SLEEVES

Using 2mm needles, cast on 84 (90, 98, 102, 106) sts.

Beg with a RS knit row, work 6 rows in st st.

Change to 3mm needles.

Continue in st st and inc 1 st at each end of 3rd and every foll 4th row to 98 (104, 112, 112, 120) sts

Work straight until sleeve measures 11cm from cast-on edge, ending with a WS row.

Shape top

Cast off 8 sts at beg of next 2 rows. 82 (88, 96, 96, 104) sts

Dec 1 st at each end of next and every foll alt row until 68 (72, 78, 76, 82) sts remain, then dec 1 st at each end of every row until 30 (32, 34, 36, 38) sts remain.

Cast off 4 sts at beg of next 4 rows.

Cast off remaining 14 (16, 18, 20, 22) sts.

COLLAR

Join shoulder seams.

Slip the first 8 sts at neck edges on to stitch holders for borders.

With WS facing, using 2mm needles, k across 30 (31, 32, 33, 34) sts from left front neck holder, pick up and k10 (11, 12, 13, 14) sts up left side of neck, k across 52 (54, 56, 58, 60) sts from back neck holder, pick up and k10 (11, 12, 13, 14) sts down right side of neck, then k across 30 (31, 32, 33, 34) sts from right front neck holder. 132 (138, 144, 150, 156) sts

Beg with a WS purl row, work 9 rows in st st.

Change to 3mm needles.

Shape back collar

Row 1 (RS): K to last 8 sts, turn.

Row 2 (WS): P to last 8 sts, turn.

Continue in this way, working 8 sts less on

every row until the row, *p to last 32 sts, turn,* has been worked.

Next row: K to end.

Next row: P to end.

Continue in st st until collar measures 10cm from beg, measured up front edge.

Inc 1 st at each end of next and every foll 4th row to 142 (148, 154, 160, 166) sts.

Work 3 more rows in st st.

Cast off.

TO MAKE UP

Slip 8 sts from stitch holders on to a 3mm needle, rejoin yarn and cast off.

Fold facings to WS and slip stitch in place.

Sew down lower edge of left border behind right, then stitch shaped edge of right border neatly into place at front. Sew in sleeves. Join side and sleeve seams.

With RS of collar facing, using a 3mm crochet hook, work 1 row of dc around collar edge. Fasten off.

Fold 5mm of fabric to WS around collar edges and slipstitch in place.

Sleeve edging: With RS facing, work 1 round of dc evenly around sleeve edge, working a multiple of 6 sts, join with ss.

Next row: *Miss 2 dc, 5tr in next dc, miss 2 dc, ss in next dc; rep from * to end.

Fasten off.

A	42.5	(45.5,	48,	50.5,	53.5)	cm
	16½	*(17¾,*	*19,*	*19¾,*	*21)*	*in*
B	17	(18,	19,	19,	20)	cm
	6¾	*(7,*	*7½,*	*7½,*	*7¾)*	*in*
C	23	(23,	23,	26,	27)	cm
	9	*(9,*	*9,*	*10¼,*	*10¾)*	*in*
D	10	cm				
	4	*in*				
E	*17*	*(18,*	*19,*	*19.5,*	*20)*	*cm*
	6¾	*(7,*	*7¼,*	*7½,*	*7¾)*	*in*
F	8	(8.5,	9,	9.5,	10)	cm
	3	*(3¼,*	*3½,*	*3¾,*	*4)*	*in*
G	6.5	cm				
	2½	*in*				
H	39	(40,	43,	45,	48)	cm
	15½	*(15¾,*	*17,*	*17¾,*	*19)*	*in*

I	32.5	(34.5,	37.5,	37.5	40)	cm
	12¾	*(13½,*	*14¾,*	*14¾,*	*15¾)*	*in*
J	11	cm				
	4¼	*in*				
K	28	(30,	32.5,	34,	35.5)	cm
	11	*(12,*	*12¾,*	*13½,*	*14)*	*in*

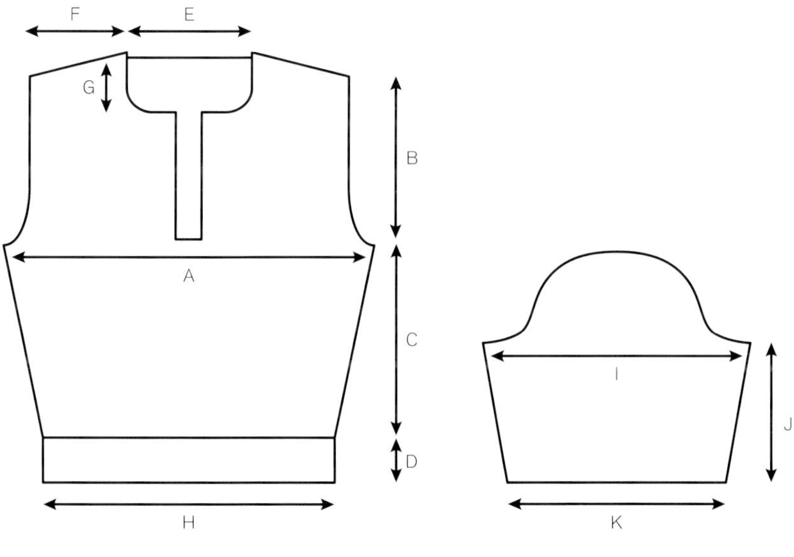

Lana Turner

1921 – 1995

One of Turner's most famous roles as a suburban mother and sexually repressed widow in *Peyton Place* (1957), which earned her an Oscar nomination, is light years away from her usual image of sexy Hollywood glamour queen. But this 'archetypal' movie princess had a difficult upbringing, often living in near poverty. However, in her mid-teens she was reputedly discovered in a drug store and propelled towards stardom.

In her early career, the public did not respond to her enthusiastically, but with the help of the legendary Hollywood publicity campaign, she was publicised as 'The Sweater Girl' in *They Won't Forget* (1937), filling an ordinary sweater as never before. All this made her a natural pin-up for US troops entering World War II.

Her popularity gained her a part in the musical *Ziegfeld Girl* (1941) with Judy Garland and Hedy Lamarr. Other films followed thick and fast and the girl from the 'Cinderella' background eventually became one of MGM's top ladies of the 1940s with box office hits such as *The Postman Always Rings Twice* (1946) and *The Three Musketeers* (1948).

The public interest in Turner was not always directed towards her movies – her private life was even more colourful. Her seven marriages and numerous love affairs were guaranteed to hold the interest of the public and did for four decades.

This smouldering *femme fatale* exuded sex and glamour whatever she wore. She imbued all clothes with her own personality: spangled gowns, tailored suits, bathrobes and bathing suits, all spelled Lana Turner.

Jane Wyman

This simple sleeveless top has a cigarette motif – once the epitome of chic – knitted from a chart, with the glowing ends embroidered in orange satin stitch. You can substitute your own motif if you prefer or knit it plain. The round neck and armholes are edged with narrow single-rib borders.

MEASUREMENTS

To fit bust:
76 (81, 86, 91, 97, 102)cm
30 (32, 34, 36, 38, 40)in

Actual measurements:
69 (74, 79, 84, 90, 95)cm

Length:
54 (54.5, 55, 55.5, 56, 56.5)cm

See schematic for full measurements.

MATERIALS

Rowan Pure Wool 4 Ply (50g balls)
   3 (4, 4, 5, 5, 6) balls in main
   colour A
Oddments of White (contrast
   colour B) for cigarette motif
Oddments of Brown (contrast
   colour C) for filter
Oddments of Orange for
   embroidering cigarette ends
A pair each of 2.75mm (UK 12)
   and 3.25mm (UK 10) knitting
   needles
Locking stitch markers
Stitch holders

TENSION

28 sts and 36 rows to 10cm over
st st using 3.25mm needles.

BACK
**Using 2.75mm needles and A, cast on 83 (89, 97, 103, 111, 117) sts.
Rib row 1: K1, *p1, k1; rep from * to end.
Rib row 2: P1, *k1, p1; rep from * to end.
Rep these 2 rows for 5cm, ending with rib row 2.
Change to 3.25mm needles.
Beg with a RS knit row, work in st st and inc 1 st at each end of 3rd and every foll 6th row to 97 (103, 111, 117, 127, 133) sts.
Work straight until back measures 33cm from cast-on edge, ending with a WS row. Place a marker at each end of last row to denote beg of armholes.**
Work straight until armholes measure 21 (21.5, 22, 22.5, 23, 23.5)cm from markers, ending with a WS row.
Shape shoulders
Cast off 12 (13, 15, 16, 18, 19) sts at beg of next 4 rows.
Break yarn and leave remaining 49 (51, 51, 53, 55, 57) sts on a holder.

FRONT
Work as given for Back from ** to **.
Beg with a RS knit row, work 14 rows in st st.
Note: When working the contrast colour patt, use separate small balls of yarn for each area of contrast colour and twist yarns together on WS of work when changing colours to avoid making a hole.
Starting with a RS knit row and working in st st throughout, reading odd numbered (knit) rows from right to left and even numbered (purl) rows from left to right, work in patt from chart as folls:
Row 1 (RS): K18 (21, 25, 28, 33, 36)A, working from chart k18A, k1B, k2A, then with A k58 (61, 65, 68, 73, 76).
Row 2: P58 (61, 65, 68, 73, 76)A, working from chart p1A, p4B, p16A, then with A, p18 (21, 25, 28, 33, 36)A.
Continue in patt from chart until row 31 has been completed.
Continuing in A only, work straight until armholes measure 15.5 (16, 16.5, 16.5, 17, 17.5)cm from markers, ending with a WS row.
Shape neck
Next row (RS): K34 (37, 41, 43, 47, 50), turn and leave remaining sts on a stitch holder.
Work on first set of sts as follows:
Dec 1 st at neck edge on every row until 24 (26, 30, 32, 36, 38) sts remain.
Work straight until front measures the same length as back to shoulders, ending at armhole edge.

Shape shoulder

Cast off 12 (13, 15, 16, 18, 19) sts at beg of next row.
Work one row.
Cast off remaining 12 (13, 15, 16, 18, 19) sts.
With RS facing, leaving first 29 (29, 29, 31, 33, 33) sts on holder, rejoin A and k to end of row. 34 (37, 41, 43, 47, 50) sts
Complete to match first side of neck.

NECKBAND

Join right shoulder seam.
With RS facing, join A to neck at left front shoulder, using 2.75mm needles, pick up and k25 (25, 26, 26, 27, 27) sts down left side of front neck, k the front neck sts from holder, pick up and k25 (25, 26, 26, 27, 27) sts up right side of front neck, then k the back neck sts from holder.
128 (130, 132, 136, 142, 144) sts
Work 5 rows in [k1, p1] rib.
Cast off in rib.

ARMHOLE BORDERS

Join left shoulder and neckband seam.
With RS facing, join A to armhole at one marker and using 2.75mm needles, pick up and k116 (120, 122, 126, 128, 132) sts evenly between markers.
Work 5 rows in [k1, p1] rib.
Cast off in rib.

TO MAKE UP

See ball band for pressing and washing details.
Join side and armhole border seams.
Using satin stitch and C, embroider tips of cigarettes.

FRONT

A (Main colour)
B (Contrast colour, white)
C (Contrast colour, brown)

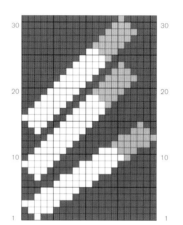

Jane Wyman
1917 – 2007

The ex-Mrs Ronald Reagan was born Sarah Jane Mayfield (later Fulks) in St Joseph, Missouri. Today, as Jane Wyman, she is best known for her powerful performance as the tragic deaf-mute in *Johnny Belinda* (1948). This film was the turning point of her career since up until then she played mostly in B films or was the heroine's best friend, playing with such big stars as Olivia de Havilland. When she eventually attained stardom (and an Oscar) for *Johnny Belinda* a new Wyman emerged; in forever playing brassy blonde roles her genuine talents had been submerged. She went on to work with Hitchcock in *Stage Fright* (1950) but they didn't hit it off – he wanted her to look plain for the part of a RADA student in London but she had other ideas.

Hollywood decided she had taste, intelligence and professionalism in the first degree. If any actress deserved an award for sheer tenacity and the will to succeed, it must surely be Jane Wyman! She went on to make movie after movie, three of the most popular being *Magnificent Obsession* (1954) and *All that Heaven Allows* (1955) both with Rock Hudson, and *Miracle in the Rain* (1956) opposite Van Johnson. Her film popularity declined at the end of the 1950s, but she went on to appear in the popular television 'soap' *Falcon Crest*.

Jane Wyman's look is very 1950s, with sharply outlined red lips setting off her slightly snub nose and well-defined angles to the face. She was always stylish and soignée, tempered with an attractive natural warmth.

A	34.5	(37,	39.5,	42,	45,	47.5) cm
	13½	*(14½,*	*15½,*	*16½,*	*17½,*	*18½) in*
B	21	(21.5,	22,	22.5,	23,	23.5) cm
	8¼	*(8½,*	*8¾,*	*8¾,*	*9,*	*9¼) in*
C	28	cm				
	11	*in*				
D	5	cm				
	2	*in*				
E	17.5	(18,	18,	19,	19.5,	20) cm
	6¾	*(7,*	*7,*	*7½,*	*7¾,*	*8) in*
F	5.5	(5.5,	5.5,	6,	6,	6) cm
	2¼	*(2¼,*	*2¼,*	*2½,*	*2½,*	*2½) in*
G	30	(32,	35,	37,	40,	42) cm
	12	*(12½,*	*13¾,*	*14½,*	*15¾,*	*16½) in*

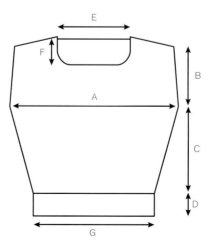

Loretta Young

The jacket-style cardigan with set-in sleeves shown on page 84 is worked in a chunky cable pattern. Instructions are given for knitting or crocheting the neck and button borders. Two tabs with button trims on the left shoulder complete the tailored look of this cardigan.

shown on page 84

MEASUREMENTS

To fit bust:
81 (86, 91, 97)cm
32 (34, 36, 38)in

Actual measurements:
93 (98, 104, 110)cm

Length to shoulders:
54 (55, 56, 57)cm

Sleeve seam:
42 (43, 44, 45)cm

See schematic for full measurements.

MATERIALS

Rowan Wool Cotton DK (50g balls)
    15 (15, 16, 16) balls
A pair each of 3mm (UK 11) and
    4mm (UK 8) knitting needles
3.5mm (UK 9) crochet hook (for
    optional crocheted borders)
Cable needle
Stitch holders
10 buttons

TENSION

26 sts and 29 rows to 10cm over cable pattern using 4mm needles.

SPECIAL ABBREVIATIONS

C4F (Cable 4 Front): Slip next 2 stitches onto cable needle and hold at front, knit the next 2 stitches, then knit the 2 stitches from the cable needle.

rtr (Raised treble): Insert hook around stem of next stitch, working from the front on right-side rows and working from the back on WS rows, then work a treble in the normal way, so that the treble is 'raised up' on the right side of the work.

BACK

Using 3mm needles, cast on 91 (95, 101,107) sts.
Rib row 1 (RS): P1, *k1, p1; rep from * to end.
Rib row 2 (WS): K1, *p1, k1; rep from * to end.
Rep these 2 rows for 10cm, ending with rib row 1.
Inc row (WS): Rib 3 (1, 2, 2), *kfb, rib 2; rep from * to last 4 (4, 3, 3) sts, kfb in next 1 (3, 1, 1) sts, rib 3 (1, 2, 2). 120 (128, 134, 142) sts
Change to 4mm needles.
Work in patt as follows:
Row 1 (RS): K to end.
Row 2 (WS): P to end.
Rows 3 and 4: As rows 1 and 2.
Row 5: K2, [C4F] 2 (3, 2, 3) times, *k2, [C4F] 3 times; rep from * to last 12 (2, 12, 2) sts, k2 (0, 2, 0), [C4F] 2 (0, 2, 0) times, k2.
Row 6: P to end.
These 6 rows form the patt.
Continue in patt until back measures 35cm from cast-on edge, ending with a WS row.
Shape armholes
Cast off 3 (4, 4, 4) sts at beg of next 2 (2, 2, 4) rows. 114 (120, 126, 126) sts
Cast off 2 (3, 3, 3) sts at beg of next 2 (2, 4, 2) rows, then cast off 2 sts at beg of next 2 (4, 2, 2) rows. 106 (106, 110, 116) sts
Dec 1 st at beg of next and every foll row until 100 (102,106,108) sts remain.

Work straight until back measures 54 (55, 56, 57)cm from cast-on edge, ending with a WS row.
Shape shoulders and neck
Cast off 7 sts at beg of next 2 rows, then 7 (7, 7, 8) sts at beg of foll 2 rows. 78 (78, 82, 86) sts
Next row: Cast off 7 (7, 8, 8) sts, patt until there are 16 (17, 18, 18) sts on needle, cast off next 26 sts, patt to end.
Work on first side of neck as follows:
Next row: Cast off 7 (7, 8, 8) sts, patt to end.
Next row: Cast off 9 (9, 10, 10) sts, patt to end.
Cast off remaining 7 (8, 8, 8) sts.
With WS facing, rejoin yarn to remaining sts and complete second side of neck to match first, reversing all shaping.

RIGHT FRONT

Using 3mm needles cast on 44 (46, 50, 52) sts.
Rib row 1 (RS): K2, * p1, k1, rep from * to end.
Rib row 2 (WS): P1, * k1, p1, rep from * to last st, k1.
Rep these 2 rows for 10cm, ending with rib row 1.
Inc row (WS): Rib 1 (7, 1, 8), *kfb. in next st, rib 2 (1, 2, 1); rep from * to last 1 (7, 1, 8) sts, kfb, rib 0 (6, 0, 7). 59 (63, 67, 71) sts

Loretta Young

Change to 4mm needles.

Work in patt as follows:

Row 1 (RS): K to end.

Row 2 (WS): P to end.

Rows 3 and 4: As rows 1 and 2.

Row 5: K1, [C4F] 1 (1, 3, 3) times, *k2, [C4F] 3 times; rep from * to last 12 (2, 12, 2) sts, k2 (0, 2, 0), [C4F] 2 (0, 2, 0) times, k2.

Row 6: P to end.

These 6 rows form the patt.

Continue in patt until work measures 35cm from cast-on edge, ending at side edge.

Shape armhole

Shape armhole as given for back, then work straight until front measures 48 (49, 50, 51)cm from cast-on edge, ending at centre front edge. 49 (50, 53, 54) sts

Shape neck

Next row: Cast off 5 sts, patt to end. 44 (45, 48, 49) sts

Cast off 3 (3, 4, 4) sts at neck edge on foll alt row, then 3 sts at beg of foll alt row and 2 sts at beg of foll 3 (3, 4, 4) alt rows. 32 (33, 33, 34) sts

Dec 1 st at neck edge at beg of foll 4 (4, 3, 3) alt rows. 28 (29, 30, 31) sts

Shape shoulder

Cast off 7 sts at beg of next row, 7 (7, 7, 8) sts at beg of foll alt row and 7 (7, 8, 8) sts at beg of foll alt row.

Work 1 row.

Cast off remaining 7 (8, 8, 8) sts.

LEFT FRONT

Work as given for right front, reversing patt on row 5 as follows:

Row 5 (RS): K2, [C4F] 2 (3, 2, 3) times, *k2, [C4F] 3 times; rep from * to last 7 (7, 1, 1) sts, k2 (2, 0, 0), [C4F] 1 (1, 0, 0) time, k1.

Continue in patt as set and complete to match right front, reversing all shaping.

SLEEVES

Using 3mm needles, cast on 50 (54, 58, 62) sts.

Work 6cm in [k1, p1] rib, ending with a RS row.

Inc row (WS): Rib 8 (1, 3, 5), *kfb, rib 1 (2, 2, 2); rep from * to last 8 (2, 4, 6) sts, kfb, rib to end. 68 (72, 76, 80) sts

Change to 4mm needles.

Work in patt as follows:

Row 1 (RS): K to end.

Row 2 (WS): P to end.

Rows 3 and 4: As rows 1 and 2.

Row 5: Kfb, k0 (2, 0, 2), [C4F] 1 (1, 2, 2) times, *k2, [C4F] 3 times; rep from * to last 7 (9, 11, 13) sts, k2, [C4F] 1 (1, 2, 2) times, k0 (2, 0, 2), kfb.

Row 6: P to end.

Continue in patt as set, increasing and working into patt 1 st at each end of 6th and every foll 4th row to 116 (120, 124, 128) sts.

Work straight until sleeve measures 42 (43, 44, 45)cm from cast-on edge, ending with a WS row.

Shape top

Cast off 3 (4, 4, 4) sts at beg of next 2 rows, then 2 sts at beg of next 12 (12, 14, 16) rows. 86 (88, 88, 88) sts

Dec 1 st at beg of next 18 (20, 20, 20) rows. 68 sts

Cast off 2 sts at beg of next 10 rows, 3 sts at beg of foll 4 rows, then 4 sts at beg of foll 4 rows.

Cast off remaining 20 sts.

CROCHETED NECKBAND

Join shoulder seams.

With RS facing, using 3.5mm crochet hook, work 85 (85, 89, 89) htr evenly around neck edge.

Next row: 3ch (counts as first tr), *1tr around next st, 1tr in next st; rep from * to last 2 sts, 1tr in each of last 2 sts.

Next row: 3ch (counts as first tr), *1tr in rtr, 1rtr around next tr; rep from * to last 2 sts, 1tr into each of last 2 sts.

Rep these 2 rows twice more.

Fasten off.

CROCHETED BUTTONHOLE BORDER

With RS facing, using 3.5mm crochet hook, work 103 (105, 107, 109)htr evenly along right front edge.

Next row: 3ch (counts as first tr), *1rtr around next st, 1tr in next st; rep from * to end.

Continuing in patt as for neckband, work 2 more rows, then work buttonholes on next row as follows:

Next row (RS): 3ch (counts as first tr), patt across 5 (7, 8, 4) sts, *2ch, miss 2 sts, patt across 11 (11, 11, 12) sts; rep from * a further 6 times, 2ch, miss 2 sts, patt to end.

Next row: Patt to end, working 2htr in 2 ch-sp.

Next row: Patt to end.

Fasten off.

CROCHETED BUTTON BORDER

Work as given for buttonhole border, omitting buttonholes.

CROCHETED TABS

Using 3.5mm hook make 15ch.

1 dc in 2nd ch from hook, 1dc in each dc to end.

Work 4 rows in dc, then fasten off.

KNITTED NECKBAND

Join shoulder seams.

With RS facing, using 3mm needles, pick up and k91 (91, 95, 95) sts evenly around neck edge.

Work in Moss st as follows:

Row 1 (WS): P1, *k1, p1; rep from * to end.

Row 2 (RS): * K1, p1; rep from * to last st, k1.

Row 3: As row 2.

Row 4: As row 1.

Rep these 4 rows until neckband measures 4cm, ending with a WS row.

Cast off in patt.

Loretta Young

KNITTED BUTTONHOLE BORDER

With RS facing, using 3mm needles, pick up and k115 (117, 121, 123) sts evenly along right front edge.

Work rows 1-4 of Moss st as given for neckband, then work rows 1 and 2 again.

Buttonhole row (WS): Patt 3 (4, 3, 4), *cast off 2 sts, patt until there are 13 (13, 14, 14) sts on needle after cast-off sts; rep from * a further 6 times, cast off 2 sts, patt to end.

Next row: Patt to end, casting on 2 sts over those cast off in previous row.

Work 5 more rows in patt.

Cast off in patt.

KNITTED BUTTON BORDER

Work as given for buttonhole border, omitting buttonholes.

KNITTED TABS

Using 3mm needles cast on 15 sts. Work 6 rows Moss st. Cast off.

TO MAKE UP

Sew in sleeves, gathering at top to fit.

Join side and sleeve seams. Sew on buttons.

Stitch top ends of tabs to left front at just below shoulder level, laying them diagonally towards the armhole.

Sew button to each of lower edges of tabs, stitching through both thicknesses to secure to front.

A	46	(49,	51,	54)	cm
	18	(19¼,	20,	21¼)	in
B	19	(20,	21,	22)	cm
	7½	(7¾,	8¼,	8¾)	in
C	25				cm
	9¾				in
D	10				cm
	4				in
E	17	(17,	18,	18)	cm
	6¾	(6¾,	7,	7)	in
F	38	(39,	40,	41)	cm
	15	(15¼,	15¾,	16)	in
G	23	(25,	26,	27)	cm
	9¼	(9¾,	10¼,	10¾)	in
H	48	(49,	50,	51)	cm
	19	(19¼,	19½,	20)	in
I	20	(20,	20.5,	20.5)	cm
	7¾	(7¾,	8,	8)	in
J	45	(46,	48,	49)	cm
	17¾	(18,	19,	19¼)	in
K	36	(37,	38,	39)	cm
	14	(14½,	15,	15½)	in
L	6				cm
	2¼				in
M	26	(28,	29,	31)	cm
	10¼	(11,	11½,	12¼)	in

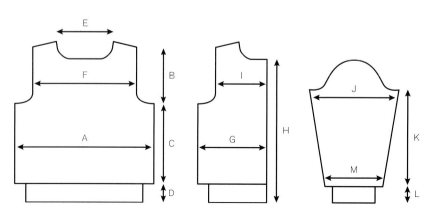

Loretta Young
1913 – 2000

Loretta Young was born in the Mormon capital, Sale Lake City, but moved to Hollywood with her mother and three sisters when she was three. She acted in her first films while still a child, but her film career began in earnest when as a teenager she was hired out as an extra to various film studios. This work culminated in a contract with Warner Brothers in 1929 where they teamed her successfully in several movies with the famous star Douglas Fairbanks Jr.

Loretta was always a glamorous and pretty woman with a face the camera loved. She was also a designer's dream, and certainly knew about clothes on and off screen. She was at her best when her roles required her to dress with style, and indeed she had many opportunities to wear flattering, extravagant costumes; in *The House of Rothschild* (1934) she looked perfect in high-waisted Regency dresses, while in *Suez* (1938) she looked equally at home playing the Countess Eugenie in full crinoline.

In her early film career she often played down-trodden, poverty-stricken heroines – but they were always beautiful and they always had class.

Her versatility and good looks, together with her accessible stylishness, ensured her a long and successful career. Her award-winning TV series *The Loretta Young Show* (1953–61) was particularly remarkable for the chic outfits that she wore. She was undoubtedly one of the aristocrats of Hollywood.

Knitting Know-How

ABBREVIATIONS

alt	Alternate
beg	Beginning
cm	Centimetre(s)
ch	Chain
ch-sp	Chain-space
dec	Decrease(d)
dc	Double crochet (US: single crochet)
foll(s)	Follows/Following
htr	Half treble crochet (US: half double)
in	Inch(es)
inc	Increase(d)
k	Knit
K1B	Knit 1 below by inserting needle into stitch below next stitch on left-hand needle, then knitting it in the usual way, letting the stitch above drop off the needle
kfb	Knit into the front and back of a stitch
M1	Make 1 stitch by picking up the loop between stitch just worked and next stitch on left-hand needle and knitting into the back of it
mm	Millimetre(s)
patt	Pattern
p	Purl
pfb	Purl into the front and back of a stitch
pwise	Purlwise
rep	Repeat
rev st st	Reverse stocking stitch – purl on RS rows, knit on WS rows
RS	Right side of work
sl	Slip
skpo	Slip 1, knit 1, pass slipstitch over
ss	Slipstitch (crochet)
st(s)	Stitch(es)
st st	Stocking stitch (stockinette) – knit on RS rows, purl on WS rows
tbl	Through the back loop
tog	Together
tr	Treble crochet (US: double crochet)
WS	Wrong side of work
yf	Yarn held forward
yb	Yarn held back
yo	Yarn over needle

TENSION

- The required tension for a 10cm square is given at the beginning of each pattern. Unless you knit with the correct tension there is little chance that your garment will come out the right size.

- To check your tension, use the stitch, yarn and needles specified in the pattern and knit a sample slightly bigger than 10cm square.

- Put the square on a flat surface, taking care not to overstretch it and, with pins, mark the number of stitches and then rows (for example 22 sts and 30 rows) required by the pattern to achieve the right tension.

- Measure the distance between the pins and, if it is not 10cm, adjust your tension.

- If, in this example, you have fewer than 22 sts to 10cm, your tension is too loose.

- Switch to smaller needles and work another square. If your tension is too tight, work another square using larger needles.

- The time taken getting your tension square right is nothing compared to unpicking an entire garment, so keep on experimenting with different needle sizes until your measurements are perfect.

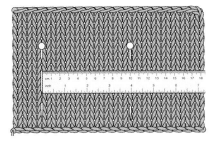

CASTING ON

1. The cable cast-on gives a firm edge that keeps its shape. Do not cast on too tightly – the stitches need to move freely. Hold yarn in your right hand about 15cm from the end and wrap it around left hand fingers. Put knitting needle tip, held in right hand, through the loop around fingers.

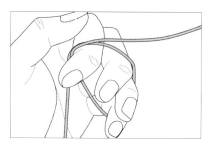

2. Wrap yarn round the needle and pull needle and the yarn wrapped around it through the loop around your hand.

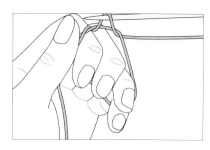

3. Keeping the yarn on the needle, slip loop off hand. Pull gently on yarn so that loop tightens around needle.

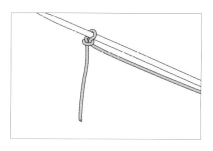

4. Hold the needle with the first loop stitch in your left hand and the other needle in your right. With the yarn's working end in your right hand, put right-hand needle's tip into stitch. Bring yarn in right hand under and around right-hand needle's point.

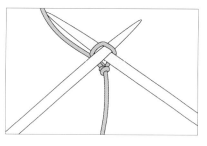

5. Pull the yarn taut so that it is wrapped around the right-hand needle tip.

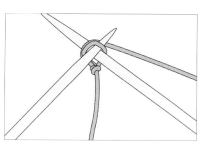

6. Bring the tip of right-hand needle and the yarn wrapped around it through the stitch and towards you.

7. Pull gently until loop is large enough to slip it over tip of left-hand needle. Take right-hand needle out of loop and pull working end of the yarn so that the loop fits snugly around the left-hand needle.

8. To cast on rest of stitches, put right-hand needle tip between last two stitches instead of through last one. Then repeat Steps 2–5 until you have required number of stitches on left-hand needle. If you find it difficult to push right-hand needle between stitches, try putting it through before tightening last stitch. With needle in place, pull last stitch tight, then work next one.

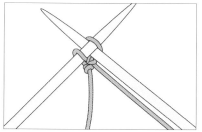

KNIT STITCH

1. From front to back, insert right-hand needle tip into first stitch on left-hand needle. Bring the yarn in right hand under right-hand needle tip. Wrap yarn over needle.

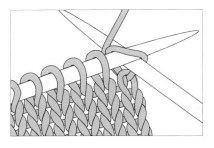

2 Bring the right-hand needle tip and yarn wrapped around it through the stitch on the left-hand needle.

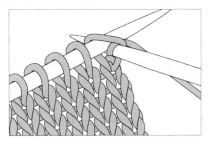

3. Pull the loop of yarn through to make a new stitch on the right-hand needle.

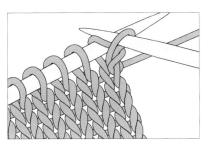

4. Slip original stitch off left-hand needle.

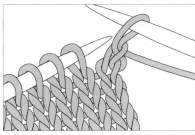

PURL STITCH

1. Start with the yarn at the front of the work, as shown. From back to front, put right-hand needle tip into first stitch on left-hand needle. Bring yarn forward and then take it over right-hand needle tip.

2. Wrap the yarn under and around the needle tip.

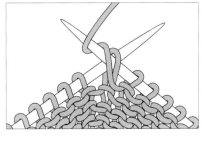

3. Bring right-hand needle tip and yarn wrapped around it backwards through stitch on left-hand needle, making sure that this stitch remains on needle.

4. Pull the loop completely through stitch, creating a new stitch on right-hand needle.

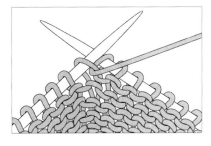

5. When it's safely through, slip original stitch off left-hand needle.

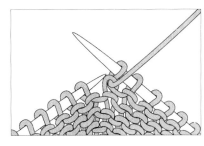

CASTING OFF

1. Using same yarn and needles as for the garment and either a knit or purl stitch, depending on whether the row would have been knitted or purled if continued, work the first two stitches.

2. Slip left-hand needle tip into the first stitch on right-hand needle. Lift it over the second stitch and drop it off needle. You have only one stitch on right-hand needle.

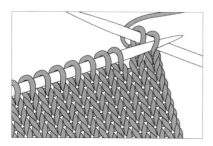

3. Knit another stitch from left-hand needle and then pass previous stitch you knitted over it. Continue until one stitch remains.

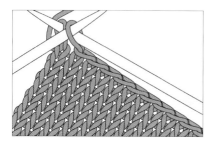

4. Cut yarn leaving a 15cm tail. Put cut end through the remaining stitch and pull it tight.

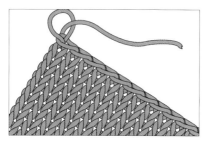

CHANGING COLOURS

This is sometimes known as Intarsia or Fair Isle method.

- When working from the charts it is necessary to use several different colours, very often within the same row.

- If there are very small areas to be worked in any of these colours, then wind off a small amount either into a small ball or onto a bobbin. This will make working with a lot of colours easier and help to stop them getting muddled.

- When joining in a new colour at the beginning of a row, insert the needle into the first stitch, make a loop in the new yarn, leaving an end to be later darned in, then place this loop over the needle and complete the stitch.

- When joining in a new colour in the middle of a row, work in the first colour to the point where the new colour is needed, then insert the needle into the next stitch and complete with the new colour in the same way as for joining in at the beginning of a row.

- When changing colour along a row, always make sure that the colour that is being used is twisted around the next colour to be used, otherwise the two stitches will not be linked together and a hole will form between them.

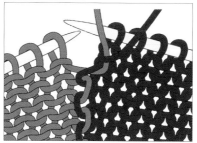

READING CHARTS

Some of the patterns in this book use charts.

- Each chart consists of a grid, sometimes the actual shape of the piece being knitted, marked up into squares.

- Each square represents one stitch and each horizontal line of squares represents one row.

- Unless otherwise given out in the instructions, the design as shown on the chart is worked in stocking stitch, all odd numbered rows being read from right to left and worked as knit stitches (RS rows) and all even numbered rows being read from left to right and worked as purl stitches (WS rows).

- Each square shows which colour yarn is to be used for that stitch.

- If on the design you are working there is only a small motif to be worked, then the chart is only given for that area of the sweater and the instructions will tell you where to place the motif within the row. All stitches either side of the chart are then worked in the main colour.

- If the chart is for the full section of the piece you are knitting, then it will usually indicate any shaping that needs to be done. If the number of squares varies at the side, armhole and neck edges, then increase or decrease that number of stitches at that point on the row that you are working.

- At the centre front neck, where there are usually quite a few stitches to be shaped, either leave the centre stitches on a holder or refer to the pattern instructions to see if it tells you to cast them off.

Embroidery

Some of the designs have added embroidery to give extra detail. The stitches featured are backstitch, French knots, satin stitch and lazy daisy stitch. Backstitch is used when just a straight line is needed, French knots are used for spots or the centres of flowers, satin stitch fills areas and lazy daisy stitches are used to form the petals and leaves of flowers.

BACKSTITCH

1. Thread the needle with required coloured yarn and fasten at back of work.

2. Bring the needle through to the right side of the fabric.

3. Insert the needle back through the fabric about 5mm to the right of where the yarn was brought through and then bring back out again about 5mm to the left of the first stitch. Draw the needle through, pulling the yarn gently.

4. Now insert the needle back into the fabric at the end of the first stitch and bring out again 5mm further along.

5. Continue in this way until the line has been completed, then fasten off securely.

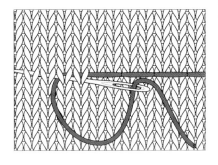

FRENCH KNOTS

1. Thread needle with required coloured yarn and fasten at back of work.

2. Bring the needle through to the right side of the fabric at the position for the knot. Take a small stitch of the fabric and wind the yarn 2, 3 or 4 times around the point of the needle (depending on how large the knot is to be).

3. Pull the needle carefully through, then insert the needle back through the fabric at the base of the knot.

4. Fasten off on the wrong side.

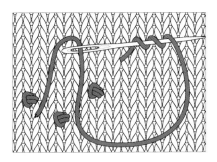

SATIN STITCH

1. Thread needle with required coloured yarn and fasten at back of work.

2. Bring the needle through to the right side of the fabric at the position for the start of the area to be covered.

3. Lay the yarn over the area to be covered and insert the needle back through the fabric to the wrong side of the work.

4. Bring the needle back through the fabric, close to the first position that the needle was brought to on the right side.

5. Insert the needle again over the area to be filled, making sure that the stitches are kept close to each other.

6. Continue in this way until the area is filled, taking care to keep the stitches at an even tension.

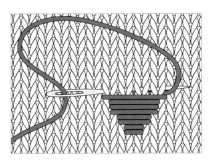

LAZY DAISY STITCH

1. Thread needle with required coloured yarn and fasten at back of work.

2. Bring needle through to the right side at the position for the start of the stitch.

3. Take a stitch, the length that you wish the petal or leaf to be, bringing the needle back through to the right side of the fabric.

4. Wind the yarn round under the needle point, then draw the needle through.

5. Finally, taking a small stitch, insert the needle back through the fabric to catch the loop into place.

6. Work several stitches in a circle to form a flower, taking care to keep all the loops the same size, making an even flower head.

BEAD EMBROIDERY

Basic stitching technique

The stab method helps to give your stitching an even tension.

1. Hold the hoop firmly and use a stabbing motion to prick the surface of the fabric with the needle.

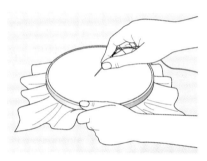

2. Bring the needle to the back of the fabric, pulling the thread through gently. Then repeat the stabbing motion to come up on the right side of your work as shown.

3. When working looped stitches, use your non-stitching thumb to hold and guide the thread around the needle as you work. This will help to prevent the thread tangling or knotting.

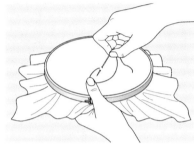

Sewing single beads
To sew on a single bead, come up through the knitting and the bead, and then take the needle back down close to the bead. Take a stitch under the knitting on the wrong side to the next bead position and repeat.

Couching
To sew several beads at once, come up through the knitting and thread a few beads onto the needle. Go down into the knitting at the end of the row of beads and take a small stitch to secure. To couch the line of beads, come up at A, over the thread between two beads, and down at B. Repeat every three or four beads.

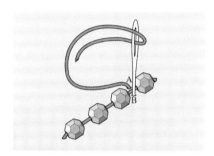

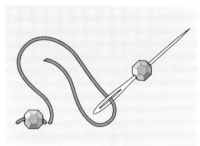

Combining beading with other embroidery stitches
If working embroidery stitches as part of the stitching, the thread will show, so use a standard embroidery thread rather than sewing thread. There are various types available, but stranded thread offers the option to use fewer strands for a finer thread when working with small beads.

Crochet stitches

Several of the garments in this book are finished with crochet edges, as there are very often no knitted equivalents. A few of the basic stitches are given here.

CHAIN

1. Make a slip loop and place on the crochet hook. Place the crochet hook in your right hand, then hold the yarn in your left hand, keeping about 5cm above the knot pulled fairly taut.

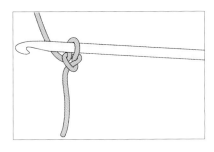

2. Hold the slip knot in your left hand and pull gently on this to form the tension. Push the hook under the yarn and back over the top so that a loop of yarn passes over the hook.

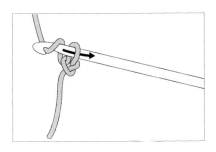

3. Draw this loop through the loop already on the hook to form one chain.

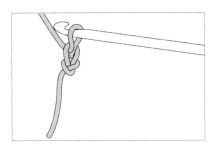

4. Repeat step 2 over and over to form the chain, pulling it down gently with the left hand to keep the tension even.

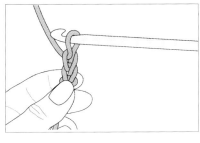

DOUBLE CROCHET

1. Make a chain the required length. Insert the hook into the 2nd chain from the hook, wind the yarn around the hook and draw a loop through.

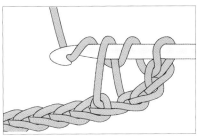

2. Wind yarn around hook again and draw through both loops on hook.

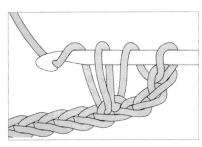

3. * Insert hook into next chain, wind yarn around hook, draw loop through, wind yarn around hook again, then draw through both loops on hook. Repeat from * to end of row.

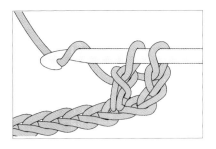

HALF TREBLE

1. Make a chain the required length. Wind yarn around hook, then insert hook in 3rd chain from hook and draw a loop through.

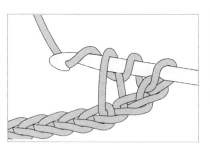

2. Wind yarn around hook again and draw through all three loops on hook.

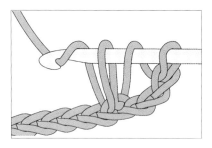

3. * Wind yarn around hook and insert hook into next chain, wind yarn around hook again, then draw through all three loops on hook. Repeat from * to end of row.

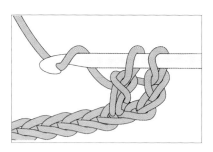

TREBLE

1. Make a chain the required length. Wind yarn around hook, then insert hook in 4th chain from hook and draw a loop through.

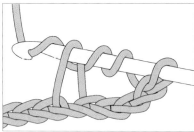

2. Wind yarn around hook again and draw through 2 of the loops on the hook, wind yarn around hook again and draw through last 2 loops on hook.

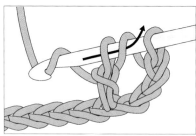

3. * Wind yarn around hook and insert hook into next chain, wind yarn around hook and draw through 2 loops, wind yarn around hook again and draw through last 2 loops. Repeat from * to end of row.

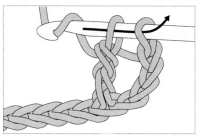

SLIPSTITCH

1. This stitch is usually used to join or neaten off the end of a row, or to work along a row, without forming any increase in the height of the fabric, to a given place.

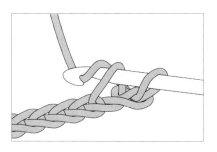

2. * Insert hook into next stitch, wind yarn around hook, draw loop through fabric and stitch on hook.

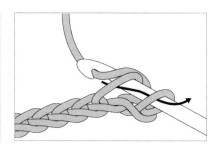

3. Repeat from * to given point.

Completing and caring for your project

After knitting, first darn or weave in all the ends securely, then for a better final look block out pieces. Once the pieces have been finished, refer to making up instructions for the order in which to assemble them. When joining seams where the pattern needs to match then the invisible seam method gives a more professional finish, but a backstitched seam is slightly easier and with care can give just as neat a finish.

FINISHING

Sewing in ends

• If the edge is not going to be sewn into a seam, then weave the end in and out of a few stitches along the edge. Skipping the last stitch, weave the end back through the stitches, then trim close to the knitting.

• If the edge is going to be seamed, then weave the end into the seam. First sew up the seam, then thread a tapestry needle with the yarn tail and weave it through a few stitches in the seam. Skipping the last stitch, weave it back through the stitches, then trim close to the knitting.

Intarsia ends

You may have a lot of ends to sew in. This can be time-consuming, but you need to do it or the knitting will unravel. Sewing in ends also gives you the opportunity to ease or tighten any irregular stitches at the beginning and end of a motif. Always sew ends into the backs of same-colour stitches or the wrong colour may show on the front.

1. Thread a tapestry needle with one end of yarn. Weave needle into the backs of four to five stitches of the same colour as the end, going through the yarn, splitting it, not under the stitches. This will provide extra friction and help stop ends working free.

2. Take the needle back through two or three of the same stitches. Pull the fabric slightly to secure the end and trim it close to the knitting.

Blocking

1. Cover a large area with a thick blanket and a piece of clean fabric, such as sheeting. Lay out each piece of the garment and pin out to shape.

2. If the yarn can be pressed (check ball band), then cover with a damp cloth and press lightly, avoiding ribbing. Do not move the iron over the fabric, but keep picking up and placing it lightly down again.

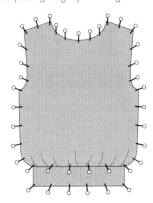

3. If the yarn cannot be pressed, then cover with a damp cloth and leave until completely dry.

MAKING UP

Invisible seam

1. Lay both pieces of fabric to be joined on a flat surface with the right sides facing. Thread the needle with matching yarn and join it to the lower edge of one of the pieces.

2. Take the needle and insert it into the centre of the first stitch at the lower edgeof the second piece of knitting. Bring the needle back up through the stitch above, so picking up the bar between the rows.

3. Pull the yarn through, then take the needle back across to the first piece of knitting and repeat. Pull the yarn gently so that the two pieces of knitting are drawn

together. Insert the needle back into the second piece of knitting, in the same place as the needle came out, and pick up the next bar above, then repeat again on the first piece of knitting.

4. Continue in this way to the top of the seam, gently pulling the yarn every few stitches to close the seam.

5. After the last stitch, fasten off securely.

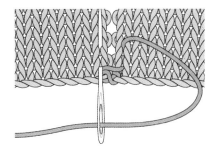

Backstitch seam

1. Place the two pieces to be joined right sides together.

2. Thread the needle with matching yarn and fasten to the beginning of the seam with a couple of stitches.

3. Insert the needle through both thicknesses and bring back out again about 5mm along the seam. Draw the needle through, pulling the yarn gently.

4. Insert the needle back into the same place as it was inserted the first time but this time bring out about 5mm further along from the last stitch. Pull the yarn through.

5. Now insert the needle back into the fabric at the end of the first stitch and bring out again 5mm further along. Continue in this way to the end of the seam, then fasten the yarn off securely.

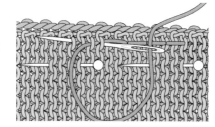

SET IN SLEEVES

This type of sleeve has a fully shaped sleeve head and the body of the garment has fully shaped armholes.

1. Sew up the sleeve and side seams.

2. Turn the body inside out and have the sleeve right side out.

3. Slip the sleeve into the armhole and pin the side seam to the sleeve seam.

4. Fold the sleeve in half to establish the top of the sleeve head and pin this to the shoulder seam.

5. Pin the rest of the sleeve in place, matching the shapings. Using backstitch, sew the sleeve in place.

AFTERCARE

After all the hard work of knitting and making up your garment it is important to wash it correctly in order to keep it looking as new. Always keep a ball band from one of the balls of yarn with which the garment was knitted, so that you can refer to the washing instructions for that yarn. If there are no washing instructions on the ball band, or if you have not kept one, then hand wash only in cool water. Either squeeze gently or give a short spin, then lay the garment flat and ease into shape. Dry flat away from heat or direct sunlight.

YARN SUPPLIERS

All the yarns in this book should be readily obtainable in the UK from good yarn suppliers.

ACKNOWLEDGEMENTS

The author and publishers acknowledge with thanks the cooperation of the following: Metro-Goldwyn-Mayer, 20th Century Fox, Warner Bros., RKO Pictures, Paramount Pictures, Goldwyn, Columbia Pictures, United Artists.

PICTURE CREDITS

All images copyright The Kobal Collection. p8 Columbia, p12 The Kobal Collection, p6 EMI/MGM, p11 Universal, p13 RKO, p14 20th Century Fox, p17 United Artists/Spurr, Melbourne, p21, 47 Paramount, p24 Warner Bros TV/Mohawk Prod, p25 Warner Bros., p35 Warner Bros./Welbourne, Scotty, p4, 64, 33 United Artists, p29, 74 MGM/Willinger, Laszlo, p39, 43, 71, 81 MGM, p53 MGM/Allan, Ted, p50 RKO/Longet, Gaston, p57 Columbia/ Cronenweth, Frank, p60 John Engstead, p61 Engstead, John, p67, 77 Warner Bros., p84 Columbia/Lippman, Irving.

Thanks to Christine and Cheryl for their research.

PAVILION

Whatever the craft, we have the book for you – just head straight to Pavilion's crafty headquarters.

Pavilioncraft.co.uk is the one-stop destination for all our fabulous craft books. Sign up for our regular newsletters and follow us on social media to receive updates on new books, competitions and interviews with our bestselling authors.

We look forward to meeting you!

www.pavilioncraft.co.uk